To Cuba and

CW00484784

Richard Henry Dana

Alpha Editions

This edition published in 2023

ISBN : 9789362096128

Design and Setting By
Alpha Editions
www.alphaedis.com
Email - info@alphaedis.com

As per information held with us this book is in Public Domain.
This book is a reproduction of an important historical work. Alpha Editions uses the
best technology to reproduce historical work in the same manner it was first
published to preserve its original nature. Any marks or number seen are left
intentionally to preserve its true form.

Contents

I

FROM MANHATTAN TO EL MORRO

The steamer is to sail at one P.M.; and, by half-past twelve, her decks are full, and the mud and snow of the pier are well trodden by men and horses. Coaches drive down furiously, and nervous passengers put their heads out to see if the steamer is off before her time; and on the decks, and in the gangways, inexperienced passengers run against everybody, and mistake the engineer for the steward, and come up the same stairs they go down, without knowing it. In the dreary snow, the newspaper vendors cry the papers, and the book vendors thrust yellow covers into your face—"Reading for the voyage, sir—five hundred pages, close print!" And that being rejected, they reverse the process of the Sibyl—with "Here's another, sir, one thousand pages, double columns." The great beam of the engine moves slowly up and down, and the black hull sways at its fasts. A motley group are the passengers. Shivering Cubans, exotics that have taken slight root in the hothouses of the Fifth Avenue, are to brave a few days of sleet and cold at sea, for the palm trees and mangoes, the cocoas and orange trees, they will be sitting under in six days, at farthest. There are Yankee shipmasters going out to join their "cotton wagons" at New Orleans and Mobile, merchants pursuing a commerce that knows no rest and no locality; confirmed invalids advised to go to Cuba to die under mosquito nets and be buried in a Potter's Field; and other invalids wisely enough avoiding our March winds; and here and there a mere vacationmaker, like myself.

Captain Bullock is sure to sail at the hour; and at the hour he is on the paddle-box, the fasts are loosed, the warp run out, the crew pull in on the warp on the port quarter, and the head swings off. No word is spoken, but all is done by signs; or, if a word is necessary, a low clear tone carries it to the listener. There is no tearing and rending escape of steam, deafening and distracting all, and giving a kind of terror to a peaceful scene; but our ship swings off, gathers way, and enters upon her voyage, in a quiet like that of a bank or counting-room, almost under a spell of silence.

The state-rooms of the "Cahawba," like those of most American sea-going steamers, are built so high above the water that the windows may be open in all but the worst of weather, and good ventilation be ensured. I have a very nice fellow for my room-mate, in the berth under me; but, in a state-room, no room-mate is better than the best; so I change my quarters to a state-room further forward, nearer "the eyes of her," which the passengers generally shun, and get one to myself, free from the rattle of the steering gear, while the delightful rise and fall of the bows, and leisurely weather roll and lee roll, cradle and nurse one to sleep.

The routine of the ship, as regards passengers, is this: a cup of coffee, if you desire it, when you turn out; breakfast at eight, lunch at twelve, dinner at three, tea at seven, and lights put out at ten.

Throughout the day, sailing down the outer edge of the Gulf Stream, we see vessels of all forms and sizes, coming in sight and passing away, as in a dioramic show. There is a heavy cotton droger from the Gulf, of 1200 tons burden, under a cloud of sail, pressing on to the northern seas of New England or Old England. Here comes a saucy little Baltimore brig, close-hauled and leaning over to it; and there, half down in the horizon, is a pile of white canvas, which the experienced eyes of my two friends, the passenger shipmasters, pronounce to be a bark, outward bound. Every passenger says to every other, how beautiful! how exquisite! That pale thin girl who is going to Cuba for her health, her brother travelling with her, sits on the settee, propped by a pillow, and tries to smile and to think she feels stronger in this air. She says she shall stay in Cuba until she gets well!

After dinner, Capt. Bullock tells us that we shall soon see the high lands of Cuba, off Matanzas, the first and highest being the Pan of Matanzas. It is clear over head, but a mist lies along the southern horizon, in the latter part of the day. The sharpest eyes detect the land, about 4 P.M., and soon it is visible to all. It is an undulating country on the coast, with high hills and mountains in the interior, and has a rich and fertile look. That height is the Pan, though we see no special resemblance, in its outline, to a loaf of bread. We are still sixty miles from Havana. We cannot reach it before dark, and no vessels are allowed to pass the Morro after the signals are dropped at sunset.

We coast the northern shore of Cuba, from Matanzas westward. There is no waste of sand and low flats, as in most of our southern states; but the fertile, undulating land comes to the sea, and rises into high hills as it recedes. "There is the Morro! and right ahead!" "Why, there is the city too! Is the city on the sea? We thought it was on a harbor or bay." There, indeed, is the Morro, a stately hill of tawny rock, rising perpendicularly from the sea, and jutting into it, with walls and parapets and towers on its top, and flags and signals flying, and the tall lighthouse just in front of its outer wall. It is not very high, yet commands the sea about it. And there is the city, on the sea-coast, indeed— the houses running down to the coral edge of the ocean. Where is the harbor, and where the shipping? Ah, there they are! We open an entrance, narrow and deep, between the beetling Morro and the Punta; and through the entrance, we see the spreading harbor and the innumerable masts. But the darkness is gathering, the sunset gun has been fired, we can just catch the dying notes of trumpets from the fortifications, and the Morro Lighthouse throws its gleam over the still sea. The little lights emerge and twinkle from the city. We are too late to enter the port, and slowly and reluctantly the ship turns her head off to seaward. The engine breathes heavily, and throws its one arm leisurely up and down; we rise and fall on the moonlit sea; the stars are near to us, or we are raised nearer to them; the Southern Cross is just above the horizon; and all night long, two streams of light lie upon the water, one of gold from the Morro, and one of silver from the moon. It is enchantment. Who can regret our delay, or wish to exchange this scene for the common, close anchorage of a harbor?

II

HAVANA: First Glimpses (I)

We are to go in at sunrise, and few, if any, are the passengers that are not on deck at the first glow of dawn. Before us lie the novel and exciting objects of the night before. The Steep Morro, with its tall sentinel lighthouse, and its towers and signal staffs and teeth of guns, is coming out into clear daylight; the red and yellow striped flag of Spain—blood and gold—floats over it. Point after point in the city becomes visible; the blue and white and yellow houses, with their roofs of dull red tiles, the quaint old Cathedral towers, and the almost endless lines of fortifications. The masts of the immense shipping rise over the headland, the signal for leave to enter is run up, and we steer in under full head, the morning gun thundering from the Morro, the trumpets braying and drums beating from all the fortifications, the Morro, the Punta, the long Cabaña, the Casa Blanca and the city walls, while the broad sun is fast rising over this magnificent spectacle.

What a world of shipping! The masts make a belt of dense forest along the edge of the city, all the ships lying head in to the street, like horses at their mangers; while the vessels at anchor nearly choke up the passage ways to the deeper bays beyond. There are the red and yellow stripes of decayed Spain; the blue, white and red—blood to the fingers' end—of La Grande Nation; the Union crosses of the Royal Commonwealth; the stars and stripes of the Great Republic, and a few flags of Holland and Portugal, of the states of northern Italy, of Brazil, and of the republics of the Spanish Main. We thread our slow and careful way among these, pass under the broadside of a ship-of-the-line, and under the stern of a screw frigate, both bearing the Spanish flag, and cast our anchor in the Regla Bay, by the side of the steamer "Karnac," which sailed from New York a few days before us.

Instantly we are besieged by boats, some loaded with oranges and bananas, and others coming for passengers and their luggage, all with awnings spread over their sterns, rowed by sallow, attenuated men, in blue and white checks and straw hats, with here and there the familiar lips and teeth, and vacant, easily-pleased face of the Negro. Among these boats comes one, from the stern of which floats the red and yellow flag with the crown in its field, and under whose awning reclines a man in a full suit of white linen, with straw hat and red cockade and a cigar. This is the Health Officer. Until he is satisfied, no one can come on board, or leave the vessel. Capt. Bullock salutes, steps down the ladder to the boat, hands his papers, reports all well— and we are pronounced safe. Then comes another boat of similar style, another man reclining under the awning with a cigar, who comes on board, is closeted with the purser, compares the passenger list with the passports, and we are declared fully passed, and general leave is given to land with our luggage at the custom-house wharf.

Now comes the war of cries and gestures and grimaces among the boatmen, in their struggle for passengers, increased manifold by the fact that there is but little language in common between the parties to the bargains, and by the boatmen being required to remain in their boats. How thin these boatmen look! You cannot get it out of your mind that they must all have had the yellow fever last summer, and are not yet fully recovered. Not only their faces, but their hands and arms and legs are thin, and their low-quartered slippers only half cover their thin yellow feet.

In the hurry, I have to hunt after the passengers I am to take leave of who go on to New Orleans:—Mr. and Mrs. Benchley, on their way to their intended new home in western Texas, my two sea captains, and the little son of my friend, who is the guest, on this voyage, of our common friend the captain, and after all, I miss the hearty hand-shake of Bullock and Rodgers. Seated under an awning, in the stern of a boat, with my trunk and carpet-bag and an unseasonable bundle of Arctic overcoat and fur cap in the bow, I am pulled by a man with an oar in each hand and a cigar in mouth, to the custom-house pier. Here is a busy scene of trunks, carpet-bags, and bundles; and up and down the pier marches a military grandee of about the rank of a sergeant or sub-lieutenant, with a preposterous strut, so out of keeping with the depressed military character of his country, and not possible to be appreciated without seeing it. If he would give that strut on the boards, in New York, he would draw full houses nightly.

Our passports are kept, and we receive a license to remain and travel in the island, good for three months only, for which a large fee is paid. These officers of the customs are civil and reasonably rapid; and in a short time my luggage is on a dray driven by a Negro, and I am in a volante, managed by a Negro postilion, and am driving through the narrow streets of this surprising city.

The streets are so narrow and the houses built so close upon them, that they seem to be rather spaces between the walls of houses than highways for travel. It appears impossible that two vehicles should pass abreast; yet they do so. There are constant blockings of the way. In some places awnings are stretched over the entire street, from house to house, and we are riding under a long tent. What strange vehicles these volantes are!—A pair of very long, limber shafts, at one end of which is a pair of huge wheels, and the other end a horse with his tail braided and brought forward and tied to the saddle, an open chaise body resting on the shafts, about one third of the way from the axle to the horse; and on the horse is a Negro, in large postilion boots, long spurs, and a bright jacket. It is an easy vehicle to ride in; but it must be a sore burden to the beast. Here and there we pass a private volante, distinguished by rich silver mountings and postilions in livery. Some have two horses, and with the silver and the livery and the long dangling traces and a look of superfluity, have rather an air of high life. In most, a gentleman is reclining, cigar in mouth; while in others, is a great puff of blue or pink muslin or cambric, extending over the sides to the shafts, topped off by a fan, with signs of a face behind it. "Calle de los Oficios," "Calle del Obispo," "Calle de San Ignacio," "Calle de Mercaderes," are on the little corner boards. Every little shop and every big shop has its title; but nowhere does the name of a keeper appear. Almost every shop advertises "por mayor y menor," wholesale and retail. What a Gil Blas-Don Quixote feeling the names of "posada," "tienda," and "cantina" give you!

There are no women walking in the streets, except negresses. Those suits of seersucker, with straw hats and red cockades, are soldiers. It is a sensible dress for the climate. Every third man, perhaps more, and not a few women, are smoking cigars or cigarritos. Here are things moving along, looking like cocks of new mown grass, under way. But presently you see the head of a horse or mule peering out from under the mass, and a tail is visible at the other end, and feet are picking their slow way over the stones. These are the carriers of green fodder, the fresh cut stalks and blades of corn; and my chance companion in the carriage, a fellow passenger by the "Cahawba," a Frenchman, who has been here before, tells me that they supply all the horses and mules in the city with their daily feed, as no hay is used. There are also mules, asses, and horses with bananas, plantains, oranges and other fruits in panniers reaching almost to the ground.

Here is the Plaza de Armas, with its garden of rich, fragrant flowers in full bloom, in front of the Governor's Palace. At the corner is the chapel erected over the spot where, under the auspices of Columbus, mass was first celebrated on the island. We are driven past a gloomy convent, past innumerable shops, past drinking places, billiard rooms, and the thick, dead walls of houses, with large windows, grated like dungeons, and large gates, showing glimpses of interior court-yards, sometimes with trees and flowers. But horses and carriages and gentlemen and ladies and slaves, all seem to use the same entrance. The windows come to the ground, and, being flush with the street, and mostly without glass, nothing but the grating prevents a passenger from walking into the rooms. And there the ladies and children sit sewing, or lounging, or playing. This is all very strange. There is evidently enough for me to see in the ten or twelve days of my stay.

But there are no costumes among the men, no Spanish hats, or Spanish cloaks, or bright jackets, or waistcoats, or open, slashed trousers, that are so picturesque in other Spanish countries. The men wear black dress coats, long pantaloons, black cravats, and many of them even submit, in this hot sun, to black French hats. The tyranny of systematic, scientific, capable, unpicturesque, unimaginative France, evidently rules over the realm of man's dress. The houses, the vehicles, the vegetation, the animals, are picturesque; to the eye of taste

> "*Every prospect pleases, and only man is vile.*"

We drove through the Puerta de Monserrate, a heavy gateway of the prevailing yellow or tawny color, where soldiers are on guard, across the moat, out upon the "Paseo de Isabel Segunda," and are now "extramuros," without the walls. The Paseo is a grand avenue running across the city from sea to bay, with two carriage-drives abreast, and two malls for foot passengers, and all lined with trees in full foliage. Here you catch a glimpse of the Morro, and there of the Presidio. This is the Teatro de Tacón; and, in front of this line of tall houses, in contrast with the almost uniform one-story buildings of the city, the volante stops. This is Le Grand's hotel.

III

HAVANA: First Glimpses (2)

To a person unaccustomed to the tropics or the south of Europe, I know of nothing more discouraging than the arrival at the inn or hotel. It is nobody's business to attend to you. The landlord is strangely indifferent, and if there is a way to get a thing done, you have not learned it, and there is no one to teach you. Le Grand is a Frenchman. His house is a restaurant, with rooms for lodgers. The restaurant is paramount. The lodging is secondary, and is left to servants. Monsieur does not condescend to show a room, even to families; and the servants, who are whites, but mere lads, have all the interior in their charge, and there are no women employed about the chambers. Antonio, a swarthy Spanish lad, in shirt sleeves, looking very much as if he never washed, has my part of the house in charge, and shows me my room. It has but one window, a door opening upon the veranda, and a brick floor, and is very bare of furniture, and the furniture has long ceased to be strong. A small stand barely holds up a basin and ewer which have not been washed since Antonio was washed, and the bedstead, covered by a canvas sacking, without mattress or bed, looks as if it would hardly bear the weight of a man. It is plain there is a good deal to be learned here. Antonio is communicative, on a suggestion of several days' stay and good pay. Things which we cannot do without, we must go out of the house to find, and those which we can do without, we must dispense with. This is odd, and strange, but not uninteresting, and affords scope for contrivance and the exercise of influence and other administrative powers. The Grand Seigneur does not mean to be troubled with anything; so there are no bells, and no office, and no clerks. He is the only source, and if he is approached, he shrugs his shoulders and gives you to understand that you have your chambers for your money and must look to the servants. Antonio starts off on an expedition for a pitcher of water and a towel, with a faint hope of two towels; for each demand involves an expedition to remote parts of the house. Then Antonio has so many rooms dependent on him, that every door is a Scylla, and every window a Charybdis, as he passes. A shrill, female voice, from the next room but one, calls "Antonio! Antonio!" and that starts the parrot in the court yard, who cries "Antonio! Antonio!" for several minutes. A deep, bass voice mutters "Antonio!" in a more confidential tone; and last of all, an unmistakably Northern voice attempts it, but ends in something between Antonio and Anthony. He is gone a good while, and has evidently had several episodes to his journey. But he is a good-natured fellow, speaks a little French, very little English, and seems anxious to do his best.

I see the faces of my New York fellow-passengers from the west gallery, and we come together and throw our acquisitions of information into a common stock, and help one another. Mr. Miller's servant, who has been here before, says there are baths and other conveniences round the corner of the street; and, sending our bundles of thin clothes there, we take advantage of the baths, with comfort. To be sure, we must go through a billiard-room, where the Creoles are playing at the tables, and the cockroaches playing under them, and through a drinking-room, and a bowling-alley; but the baths are built in the open yard, protected by blinds, well ventilated, and well supplied with water and toilet apparatus.

With the comfort of a bath, and clothed in linen, with straw hats, we walk back to Le Grand's, and enter the restaurant, for breakfast—the breakfast of the country, at 10 o'clock. Here is a scene so pretty as quite to make up for the defects of the chambers. The restaurant with cool marble floor, walls twenty-four feet high, open rafters painted blue, great windows open to the floor and looking into the Paseo, and the floor nearly on a level with the street, a light breeze fanning the thin curtains, the little tables, for two or four, with clean, white cloths, each with its pyramid of great red oranges and its fragrant bouquet—the gentlemen in white pantaloons and jackets and white stockings, and the ladies in fly-away muslins, and hair in the sweet neglect of the morning toilet, taking their leisurely breakfasts of fruit and claret, and omelette and Spanish mixed dishes, (ollas,) and café noir. How airy and ethereal it seems! They are birds, not substantial men and women. They eat ambrosia and drink nectar. It must be that they fly, and live in nests, in the tamarind trees. Who can eat a hot, greasy breakfast of cakes and gravied meats, and in a close room, after this?

I can truly say that I ate, this morning, my first orange; for I had never before eaten one newly gathered, which had ripened in the sun, hanging on the tree. We call for the usual breakfast, leaving the selection to the waiter; and he brings us fruits, claret, omelette, fish fresh from the sea, rice excellently cooked, fried plantains, a mixed dish of meat and vegetables (olla), and coffee. The fish, I do not remember its name, is boiled, and has the colors of the rainbow, as it lies on the plate. Havana is a good fishmarket; for it is as open to the ocean as Nahant, or the beach at Newport; its streets running to the blue sea, outside the harbor, so that a man may almost throw his line from the curb-stone into the Gulf Stream.

After breakfast, I take a volante and ride into the town, to deliver my letters. Three merchants whom I call upon have palaces for their business. The entrances are wide, the staircases almost as stately as that of Stafford House, the floors of marble, the panels of porcelain tiles, the rails of iron, and the rooms over twenty feet high, with open rafters, the doors and windows colossal, the furniture rich and heavy; and there sits the merchant or banker, in white pantaloons and thin shoes and loose white coat and narrow necktie, smoking a succession of cigars, surrounded by tropical luxuries and tropical protections. In the lower story of one of these buildings is an exposition of silks, cotton and linens, in a room so large that it looked like a part of the Great Exhibition in Hyde Park. At one of these counting-palaces, I met Mr. Theodore Parker and Dr. S. G. Howe, of Boston, who preceded me, in the "Karnac." Mr. Parker is here for his health, which has caused anxiety to his friends lest his weakened frame should no longer support the strong intellectual machinery, as before. He finds Havana too hot, and will leave for Santa Cruz by the first opportunity. Dr. Howe likes the warm weather. It is a comfort to see him—a benefactor of his race, and one of the few heroes we have left to us, since Kane died.

The Bishop of Havana has been in delicate health, and is out of town, at Jesús del Monte, and Miss M—— is not at home, and the Señoras F—— I failed to see this morning; but I find a Boston young lady, whose friends were desirous I should see her, and who was glad enough to meet one so lately from her home. A clergyman to whom, also, I had letters, is gone into the country, without much hope of improving his health. Stepping into a little shop to buy a plan of Havana, my name is called, and there is my hero's wife, the accomplished author and conversationist, whom it is an exhilaration to meet anywhere, much more in a land of strangers. Dr. and Mrs. Howe and Mr. Parker are at the Cerro, a pretty and cool place in the suburbs, but are coming in to Mrs. Almy's boarding-house, for the convenience of being in the city, and for nearness to friends, and the comforts of something like American or English housekeeping.

In the latter part of the afternoon, from three o'clock, our parties are taking dinner at Le Grand's. The little tables are again full, with a fair complement of ladies. The afternoon breeze is so strong that the draught of air, though it is hot air, is to be avoided. The passers-by almost put their faces into the room, and the women and children of the poorer order look wistfully in upon the luxurious guests, the colored glasses, the red wines, and the golden fruits. The Opera troupe is here, both the singers and the ballet; and we have Gazzaniga, Lamoureux, Max Maretzek and his sister, and others, in this house, and Adelaide Phillips at the next door, and the benefit of a rehearsal, at nearly all hours of the day, of operas that the Habaneros are to rave over at night.

I yield to no one in my admiration of the Spanish as a spoken language, whether in its rich, sonorous, musical, and lofty style, in the mouth of a man who knows its uses, or in the soft, indolent, languid tones of a woman, broken by an occasional birdlike trill—

"*With wanton heed, and giddy cunning,*

The melting voice through mazes running"

but I do not like it as spoken by the common people of Cuba, in the streets. Their voices and intonations are thin and eager, very rapid, too much in the lips, and, withal, giving an impression of the passionate and the childish combined; and it strikes me that the tendency here is to enfeeble the language, and take from it the openness of the vowels and the strength of the harder consonants. This is the criticism of a few hours' observation, and may not be just; but I have heard the same from persons who have been longer acquainted with it. Among the well educated Cubans, the standard of Castilian is said to be kept high, and there is a good deal of ambition to reach it.

After dinner, walked along the Paseo de Isabel Segunda, to see the pleasure-driving, which begins at about five o'clock, and lasts until dark. The most common carriage is the volante, but there are some carriages in the English style, with servants in livery on the box. I have taken a fancy for the strange-looking two-horse volante. The postilion, the long, dangling traces, the superfluousness of a horse to be ridden by the man that guides the other, and the prodigality of silver, give the whole a look of style that eclipses, the neat appropriate English equipage. The ladies ride in full dress, décolletées, without hats. The servants on the carriages are not all Negroes. Many of the drivers are white. The drives are along the Paseo de Isabel, across the Campo del Marte, and then along the Paseo de Tacón, a beautiful double avenue, lined with trees, which leads two or three miles, in a straight line, into the country.

At 8 o'clock, drove to the Plaza de Armas, a square in front of the governor's house, to hear the Retreta, at which a military band plays for an hour, every evening. There is a clear moon above, and a blue field of glittering stars; the air is pure and balmy; the band of fifty or sixty instruments discourses most eloquent music under the shade of palm trees and mangoes; the walks are filled with promenaders, and the streets around the square lined with carriages, in which the ladies recline, and receive the salutations and visits of the gentlemen. Very few ladies walk in the square, and those probably are strangers. It is against the etiquette for ladies to walk in public in Havana.

I walk leisurely home, in order to see Havana by night. The evening is the busiest season for the shops. Much of the business of shopping is done after gas lighting. Volantes and coaches are driving to and fro, and stopping at the shop doors, and attendants take their goods to the doors of the carriages. The watchmen stand at the corners of the streets, each carrying a long pike and a lantern. Billiard-rooms and cafés are filled, and all who can walk for pleasure will walk now. This is also the principal time for paying visits.

There is one strange custom observed here in all the houses. In the chief room, rows of chairs are placed, facing each other, three or four or five in each line, and always running at right angles with the street wall of the house. As you pass along the street, you look up this row of chairs. In these, the family and the visitors take their seats, in formal order. As the windows are open, deep, and large, with wide gratings and no glass, one has the inspection of the interior arrangement of all the front parlors of Havana, and can see what every lady wears, and who is visiting her.

IV

HAVANA: Prisoners and Priests

If mosquito nets were invented for the purpose of shutting mosquitoes in with you, they answer their purpose very well. The beds have no mattresses, and you lie on the hard sacking. This favors coolness and neatness. I should fear a mattress, in the economy of our hotel, at least. Where there is nothing but an iron frame, canvas stretched over it, and sheets and a blanket, you may know what you are dealing with.

The clocks of the churches and castles strike the quarter hours, and at each stroke the watchmen blow a kind of boatswain's whistle, and cry the time and the state of the weather, which, from their name (serenos), should be always pleasant.

I have been advised to close the shutters at night, whatever the heat, as the change of air that often takes place before dawn is injurious; and I notice that many of the bedrooms in the hotel are closed, both doors and shutters, at night. This is too much for my endurance, and I venture to leave the air to its course, not being in the draught. One is also cautioned not to step with bare feet on the floor, for fear of the nigua (or chigua), a very small insect, that is said to enter the skin and build tiny nests, and lay little eggs that can only be seen by the microscope, but are tormenting and sometimes dangerous. This may be excessive caution, but it is so easy to observe, that it is not worth while to test the question.

There are streaks of a clear dawn; it is nearly six o'clock, the cocks are crowing, and the drums and trumpets sounding. We have been told of sea-baths, cut in the rock, near the Punta, at the foot of our Paseo. I walk down, under the trees, toward the Presidio. What is this clanking sound? Can it be cavalry, marching on foot, their sabres rattling on the pavement? No, it comes from that crowd of poor-looking creatures that are forming in files in front of the Presidio. It is the chain-gang! Poor wretches! I come nearer to them, and wait until they are formed and numbered and marched off. Each man has an iron band riveted round his ankle, and another round his waist, and the chain is fastened, one end into each of these bands, and dangles between them, clanking with every movement. This leaves the wearers free to use their arms, and, indeed, their whole body, it being only a weight and a badge and a note for discovery, from which they cannot rid themselves. It is kept on them day and night, working, eating, or sleeping. In some cases, two are chained together. They have passed their night in the Presidio (the great prison and garrison), and are marshalled for their day's toil in the public streets and on the public works, in the heat of the sun. They look thoroughly wretched. Can any of these be political offenders? It is said that Carlists, from

Old Spain, worked in this gang. Sentence to the chain-gang in summer, in the case of a foreigner, must be nearly certain death.

Farther on, between the Presidio and the Punta, the soldiers are drilling; and the drummers and trumpeters are practising on the rampart of the city walls.

A little to the left, in the Calzada de San Lázaro, are the Baños de Mar. These are boxes, each about twelve feet square and six or eight feet deep, cut directly into the rock which here forms the sea-line, with steps of rock, and each box having a couple of portholes through which the waves of this tideless shore wash in and out. This arrangement is necessary, as sharks are so abundant that bathing in the open sea is dangerous. The pure rock, and the flow and reflow, make these bathing-boxes very agreeable, and the water, which is that of the Gulf Stream, is at a temperature of 72 degrees. The baths are roofed over, and partially screened on the inside, but open for a view out, on the side towards the sea; and as you bathe, you see the big ships floating up the Gulf Stream, that great highway of the Equinoctial world. The water stands at depths of from three to five feet in the baths; and they are large enough for short swimming. The bottom is white with sand and shells. These baths are made at the public expense, and are free. Some are marked for women, some for men, and some "por la gente de color." A little further down the Calzada, is another set of baths, and further out in the suburbs, opposite the Beneficencia, are still others.

After bath, took two or three fresh oranges, and a cup of coffee, without milk; for the little milk one uses with coffee must not be taken with fruit here, even in winter.

To the Cathedral, at 8 o'clock, to hear mass. The Cathedral, in its exterior, is a plain and quaint old structure, with a tower at each angle of the front; but within, it is sumptuous. There is a floor of variegated marble, obstructed by no seats or screens, tall pillars and rich frescoed walls, and delicate masonry of various colored stone, the prevailing tint being yellow, and a high altar of porphyry. There is a look of the great days of Old Spain about it; and you think that knights and nobles worshipped here and enriched it from their spoils and conquests. Every new eye turns first to the place within the choir, under that alto-relief, behind that short inscription, where, in the wall of the chancel, rest the remains of Christopher Columbus. Borne from Valladolid to Seville, from Seville to San Domingo, and from San Domingo to Havana, they at last rest here, by the altar side, in the emporium of the Spanish Islands. "What is man that thou art mindful of him!" truly and humbly says the Psalmist; but what is man, indeed, if his fellow men are not mindful of such a man as this! The creator of a hemisphere! It is not often we feel that monuments are surely deserved, in their degree and to the extent of their utterance. But when, in the New World, on an island of that group which he gave to civilized man, you stand before this simple monumental slab, and know that all of him that man can gather up, lies behind it, so overpowering is the sense of the greatness of his deeds, that you feel relieved that no attempt has been made to measure it by any work of man's hands. The little there is, is so inadequate, that you make no comparison. It is a mere finger-point, the *hic jacet*, the *sic itur*.

The priests in the chancel are numerous, perhaps twenty or more. The service is chanted with no aid of instruments, except once the accompaniment of a small and rather disordered organ, and chanted in very loud and often harsh and blatant tones, which reverberate from the marble walls, with a tiresome monotony of cadence. There is a degree of ceremony in the placing, replacing, and carrying to and fro of candles and crucifixes, and swinging of censers, which the Roman service as practised in the United States does not give. The priests seem duly attentive and reverent in their manner, but I cannot say as much for the boys, of whom there were three or four, gentlemen-like looking lads, from the college, doing service as altar boys. One of these, who seemed to have the lead, was strikingly careless and irreverent in his manner; and when he went about the chancel, to incense all who were there, and to give to each the small golden vessel to kiss, (containing, I suppose a relic), he seemed as if he were counting his playmates out for a game, and flinging the censer at them and snubbing their noses with the golden vessel.

There were only about half a dozen persons at mass, beside those in the chancel; and all but one of these were women, and of the women two were Negroes. The women walk in, veiled, drop down on the bare pavement, kneeling or sitting, as the service requires or permits. A Negro woman, with devout and even distressed countenance, knelt at the altar rail, and one pale-eyed priest, in cassock, who looked like an American or Englishman, knelt close by a pillar. A file of visitors, American or English women, with an escort of gentlemen, came in and sat on the only benches, next the columns; and when the Host was elevated, and a priest said to them, very civilly, in English, "Please to kneel down," they neither knelt nor stood, nor went away, but kept their seats.

After service, the old sacristan, in blue woollen dress, showed all the visitors the little chapel and the cloisters, and took us beyond the altar to the mural tomb of Columbus, and though he was liberally paid, haggled for two reals more.

In the rear of the Cathedral is the Seminario, or college for boys, where also men are trained for the priesthood. There are cloisters and a pleasant garden within them.

V

HAVANA: Olla Podrida

Breakfast, and again the cool marble floor, white-robed tables, the fruits and flowers, and curtains gently swaying, and women in morning toilets. Besides the openness to view, these rooms are strangely open to ingress. Lottery-ticket vendors go the rounds of the tables at every meal, and so do the girls with tambourines for alms for the music in the street. As there is no coin in Cuba less than the medio, 6¼ cents, the musicians get a good deal or nothing. The absence of any smaller coin must be an inconvenience to the poor, as they must often buy more than they want, or go without. I find silver very scarce here. It is difficult to get change for gold, and at public places notices are put up that gold will not be received for small payments. I find the only course is to go to one of the Cambios de Moneda, whose signs are frequent in the streets, and get a half doubloon changed into reals and pesetas, at four per cent discount, and fill my pockets with small silver.

Spent the morning, from eleven o'clock to dinner-time, in my room, writing and reading. It is too hot to be out with comfort. It is not such a morning as one would spend at the St. Nicholas, or the Tremont, or at Morley's or Meurice's. The rooms all open into the court-yard, and the doors and windows, if open at all, are open to the view of all passers-by. As there are no bells, every call is made from the veranda rail, down into the court-yard, and repeated until the servant answers, or the caller gives up in despair. Antonio has a compeer and rival in Domingo, and the sharp voice of the woman in the next room but one, who proves to be a subordinate of the opera troupe, is calling out,"Do-meen-go! Do-meen-go!" and the rogue is in full sight from our side, making significant faces, until she changes her tune to "Antonio! Antonio! adónde está Domingo?" But as she speaks very little Spanish, and Antonio very little French, it is not difficult for him to get up a misapprehension, especially at the distance of two stories; and she is obliged to subside for a while, and her place is supplied by the parrot. She is usually unsuccessful, being either unreasonable, or bad pay. The opera troupe are rehearsing in the second flight, with doors and windows open. And throughout the hot middle day, we hear the singing, the piano, the parrot, and the calls and parleys with the servants below. But we can see the illimitable sea from the end of the piazza, blue as indigo; and the strange city is lying under our eye, with its strange blue and white and yellow houses, with their roofs of dull red tiles, its strange tropical shade-trees, and its strange vehicles and motley population, and the clangor of its bells, and the high-pitched cries of the vendors in its streets.

Going down stairs at about eleven o'clock, I find a table set in the front hall, at the foot of the great staircase, and there, in full view of all who come or go, the landlord and his entire establishment, except the slaves and coolies, are at breakfast. This is done every day. At the café round the corner, the family with their white, hired servants, breakfast and dine in the hall, through which all the customers of the place must go to the baths, the billiard rooms, and the bowling-alleys. Fancy the manager of the Astor or Revere, spreading a table for breakfast and dinner in the great entry, between the office and the front door, for himself and family and servants!

Yesterday and to-day I noticed in the streets and at work in houses, men of an Indian complexion, with coarse black hair. I asked if they were native Indians, or of mixed blood. No, they are the coolies! Their hair, full grown, and the usual dress of the country which they wore, had not suggested to me the Chinese; but the shape and expression of the eye make it plain. These are the victims of the trade, of which we hear so much. I am told there are 200,000 of them in Cuba, or, that so many have been imported, and all within seven years. I have met them everywhere, the newly-arrived, in Chinese costume, with shaved heads, but the greater number in pantaloons and jackets and straw hats, with hair full grown. Two of the cooks at our hotel are coolies. I must inform myself on the subject of this strange development of the domination of capital over labor. I am told there is a mart of coolies in the Cerro. This I must see, if it is to be seen.

After dinner drove out to the Jesús del Monte, to deliver my letter of introduction to the Bishop. The drive, by way of the Calzada de Jesús del Monte, takes one through a wretched portion, I hope the most wretched portion, of Havana, by long lines of one story wood and mud hovels, hardly habitable even for Negroes, and interspersed with an abundance of drinking shops. The horses, mules, asses, chickens, children, and grown people use the same door; and the back yards disclose heaps of rubbish. The looks of the men, the horses tied to the door-posts, the mules with their panniers of fruits and leaves reaching to the ground, all speak of Gil Blas, and of what we have read of humble life in Spain. The little Negro children go stark naked, as innocent of clothing as the puppies. But this is so all over the city. In the front hall of Le Grand's, this morning, a lady, standing in a full dress of spotless white, held by the hand a naked little Negro boy, of two or three years old, nestling in black relief against the folds of her dress.

Now we rise to the higher grounds of Jesús del Monte. The houses improve in character. They are still of one story, but high and of stone, with marble floors and tiled roofs, with court-yards of grass and trees, and through the gratings of the wide, long, open windows, I see the decent furniture, the double, formal row of chairs, prints on the walls, and well-dressed women maneuvering their fans.

As a carriage with a pair of cream-colored horses passed, having two men within, in the dress of ecclesiastics, my driver pulled up and said that was the Bishop's carriage, and that he was going out for an evening drive. Still, I must go on; and we drive to his house. As you go up the hill, a glorious view lies upon the left. Havana, both city and suburbs, the Morro with its batteries and lighthouse, the ridge of fortifications called the Cabaña and Casa Blanca, the Castle of Atares, near at hand, a perfect truncated cone, fortified at the top—the higher and most distant Castle of Príncipe,

"And, poured round all,

Old Ocean's gray and melancholy waste"—

No! Not so! Young Ocean, the Ocean of to-day! The blue, bright, healthful, glittering, gladdening, inspiring Ocean! Have I ever seen a city view so grand? The view of Quebec from the foot of the Montmorenci Falls, may rival, but does not excel it. My preference is for this; for nothing, not even the St. Lawrence, broad and affluent as it is, will make up for the living sea, the boundless horizon, the dioramic vision of gliding, distant sails, and the open arms and motherly bosom of the harbor, "with handmaid lamp attending":— our Mother Earth, forgetting never the perils of that gay and treacherous world of waters, its change of moods, its "strumpet winds"—ready is she at all times, by day or by night, to fold back to her bosom her returning sons, knowing that the sea can give them no drink, no food, no path, no light, nor bear up their foot for an instant, if they are sinking in its depths.

The regular episcopal residence is in town. This is only a house which the Bishop occupies temporarily, for the sake of his health. It is a modest house of one story, standing very high, with a commanding view of city, harbor, sea, and suburbs. The floors are marble, and the roof is of open rafters, painted blue, and above twenty feet in height; the windows are as large as doors, and the doors as large as gates. The mayordomo shows me the parlor, in which are portraits in oil of distinguished scholars and missionaries and martyrs.

On my way back to the city, I direct the driver to avoid the disagreeable road by which we came out, and we drive by a cross road, and strike the Paseo de Tacón at its outer end, where is a fountain and statue, and a public garden of the most exquisite flowers, shrubs, and trees, and around them are standing, though it is nearly dark, files of carriages waiting for the promenaders, who are enjoying a walk in the garden. I am able to take the entire drive of the Paseo. It is straight, very wide, with two carriageways and two footways, with rows of trees between, and at three points has a statue and a fountain. One of these statues, if I recollect aright, is of Tacón; one of a Queen of Spain; and one is an allegorical figure. The Paseo is two or three miles in length;

reaching from the Campo de Marte, just outside the walls, to the last statue and public garden, on gradually ascending ground, and lined with beautiful villas, and rich gardens full of tropical trees and plants. No city in America has such an avenue as the Paseo de Tacón. This, like most of the glories of Havana, they tell you they owe to the energy and genius of the man whose name it bears.—I must guard myself, by the way, while here, against using the words America and American, when I mean the United States and the people of our Republic; for this is America also; and they here use the word America as including the entire continent and islands, and distinguish between Spanish and English America, the islands and the main.

The Cubans have a taste for prodigality in grandiloquent or pretty names. Every shop, the most humble, has its name. They name the shops after the sun and moon and stars; after gods and goddesses, demi-gods and heroes; after fruits and flowers, gems and precious stones; after favorite names of women, with pretty, fanciful additions; and after all alluring qualities, all delights of the senses, and all pleasing affections of the mind. The wards of jails and hospitals are each known by some religious or patriotic designation; and twelve guns in the Morro are named for the Apostles. Every town has the name of an apostle or saint, or of some sacred subject. The full name of Havana, in honor of Columbus, is San Cristóbal de la Habana; and that of Matanzas is San Carlos Alcázar de Matanzas. It is strange that the island itself has defied all the Spanish attempts to name it. It has been solemnly named Juana, after the daughter of Ferdinand and Isabella; then Ferdinandina, after Ferdinand himself; then Santiago, and, lastly, Ave María; but it has always fallen back upon the original Indian name of Cuba. And the only compensation to the hyperbolical taste of the race is that they decorate it, on state and ceremonious occasions, with the musical prefix of "La siempre fidelísima Isla de Cuba."

At 7.30 P.M. went with my New York fellow-passengers to hear an opera, or, more correctly, to see the people of Havana at an opera. The Teatro de Tacón is closed for repairs. This is unfortunate, as it is said by some to be the finest theater, and by all to be one of the three finest theaters in the world. This, too, is attributed to Tacón; although it is said to have been a speculation of a clever pirate turned fish-dealer, who made a fortune by it. But I like well enough the Teatro de Villanueva. The stage is deep and wide, the pit high and comfortable, and the boxes light and airy and open in front, with only a light tracery of iron to support the rails, leaving you a full view of the costumes of the ladies, even to their slippers. The boxes are also separated from the passage-ways in the rear, only by wide lattice work; so that the promenaders between the acts can see the entire contents of the boxes at one view; and the ladies dress and sit and talk and use the fan with a full sense that they are under the inspection of a "committee of the whole house." They are all in full dress, décolletées, without hats. It seemed, to my fancy, that the mature women were divisible into two classes, distinctly marked and with few intermediates—the obese and the shrivelled. I suspect that the effect of time in this climate is to produce a decided result in the one direction or the other. But a single night's view at an opera is very imperfect material for an induction, I admit. The young ladies had, generally, full figures, with tapering fingers and well-rounded arms; yet there were some in the extreme contrast of sallow, bilious, sharp countenances, with glassy eyes. There is evidently great attention to manner, to the mode of sitting and moving, to the music of the voice in speaking, the use of the hands and arms, and, perhaps it may be ungallant to add, of the eyes.

The Governor-General, Concha (whose title is, strictly, Capitan-General), with his wife and two daughters, and two aides-de-camp, is in the Vice-regal box, hung with red curtains, and surmounted by the royal arms. I can form no opinion of him from his physiognomy, as that is rather heavy, and gives not much indication.

Between the acts, I make, as all the gentlemen do, the promenade of the house. All parts of it are respectable, and the regulations are good. I notice one curious custom, which I am told prevails in all Spanish theaters. As no women sit in the pit, and the boxes are often hired for the season, and are high-priced, a portion of an upper tier is set apart for those women and children who cannot or do not choose to get seats in the boxes. Their quarter is separated from the rest of the house by gates, and is attended by two or three old women, with a man to guard the entrance. No men are admitted among them, and their parents, brothers, cousins and beaux are allowed only to come to the door, and must send in refreshments, and even a cup of water, by the hands of the dueñas.

Military, on duty, abound at the doors and in the passage-ways. The men to-night are of the regiment of Guards, dressed in white. There are enough of them to put down a small insurrection, on the spot. The singers screamed well enough, and the play was a poor one, "María de Rohan," but the prima donna, Gazzaniga, is a favorite, and the excitable Cubans shout and scream, and throw bouquets, and jump on the benches, and, at last, present her with a crown, wreathed with flowers, and with jewels of value attached to it. Miss Adelaide Phillips is here, too, and a favorite, and has been crowned, they say; but she does not sing to-night.

VI

HAVANA: A Social Sunday

To-morrow, I am to go, at eight o'clock either to the church of San Domingo, to hear the military mass, or to the Jesuit church of Belén; for the service of my own church is not publicly celebrated, even at the British consulate, no service but the Roman Catholic being tolerated on the island.

To-night there is a public máscara (mask ball) at the great hall, next door to Le Grand's. My only window is by the side of the numerous windows of the great hall, and all these are wide open; and I should be stifled if I were to close mine. The music is loud and violent, from a very large band, with kettle drums and bass drums and trumpets; and because these do not make noise and uproar enough, leather bands are snapped, at the turns in the tunes. For sleeping, I might as well have been stretched on the bass drum. This tumult of noises, and the heat are wearing and oppressive beyond endurance, as it draws on past midnight, to the small hours; and the servants in the court of the hall seem to be tending at tables of quarrelling men, and to be interminably washing and breaking dishes. After several feverish hours, I light a match and look at my watch. It is nearly five o'clock in the morning. There is an hour to daylight—and will this noise stop before then? The city clocks struck five; the music ceased; and the bells of the convents and monasteries tolled their matins, to call the nuns and monks to their prayers and to the bedsides of the sick and dying in the hospitals, as the maskers go home from their revels at this hideous hour of Sunday morning. The servants ceased their noises, the cocks began to crow and the bells to chime, the trumpets began to bray, and the cries of the streets broke in before dawn, and I dropped asleep just as I was thinking sleep past hoping for; when I am awakened by a knocking at the door, and Antonio calling, "Usted! Usted! Un caballero quiere ver á Usted!" to find it half-past nine, the middle of the forenoon, and an ecclesiastic in black dress and shovel hat, waiting in the passage-way, with a message from the bishop.

His Excellency regrets not having seen me the day before, and invites me to dinner at three o'clock, to meet three or four gentlemen, an invitation which I accept with pleasure.

I am too late for the mass, or any other religious service, as all the churches close at ten o'clock. A tepid, soothing bath, at "Los baños públicos," round the corner, and I spend the morning in my chamber. As we are at breakfast, the troops pass by the Paseo, from the mass service. Their gait is quick and easy, with swinging arms, after the French fashion. Their dress is seersucker, with straw hats and red cockades: the regiments being distinguished by the color of the cloth on the cuffs of the coat, some being yellow, some green, and some blue.

Soon after two o'clock, I take a carriage for the bishop's. On my way out I see that the streets are full of Spanish sailors from the men-of-war, ashore for a holiday, dressed in the style of English sailors, with wide duck trousers, blue jackets, and straw hats, with the name of their ship on the front of the hat. All business is going on as usual, and laborers are at work in the streets and on the houses.

The company consists of the bishop himself, the Bishop of Puebla de los Ángeles in Mexico, Father Yuch, the rector of the Jesuit College, who has a high reputation as a man of intellect, and two young ecclesiastics. Our dinner is well cooked, and in the Spanish style, consisting of fish, vegetables, fruits, and of stewed light dishes, made up of vegetables, fowls and other meats, a style of cooking well adapted to a climate in which one is very willing to dispense with the solid, heavy cuts of an English dinner.

The Bishop of Puebla wore the purple, the Bishop of Havana a black robe with a broad cape, lined with red, and each wore the Episcopal cross and ring. The others were in simple black cassocks. The conversation was in French; for, to my surprise, none of the company could speak English; and being allowed my election between French and Spanish, I chose the former, as the lighter infliction on my associates.

I am surprised to see what an impression is made on all classes in this country by the pending "Thirty Millions Bill" of Mr. Slidell. It is known to be an Administration measure, and is thought to be the first step in a series which is to end in an attempt to seize the island. Our steamer brought oral intelligence that it had passed the Senate, and it was so announced in the Diario of the day after our arrival, although no newspaper that we brought so stated it. Not only with these clergymen, but with the merchants and others whom I have met since our arrival, foreigners as well as Cubans, this is the absorbing topic. Their future seems to be hanging in doubt, depending on the action of our government, which is thought to have a settled purpose to acquire the island. I suggested that it had not passed the Senate, and would not pass the House; and, at most, was only an authority to the President to make an offer that would certainly be refused. But they looked beyond the form of the act, and regarded it as the first move in a plan, of which, although they could not entirely know the details, they thought they understood the motive.

These clergymen were well informed as to the state of religion in the United States, the relative numbers and force of the various denominations, and their doctrinal differences; the reputations of Brownson, Parker, Beecher, and others; and most minutely acquainted with the condition of their own church in the United States, and with the chief of its clergy. This acquaintance is not attributable solely to their unity of organization, and to the consequent interchange of communication, but largely also to the tie of a common education at the Propaganda or St. Sulpice, the catalogues of whose alumni are familiar to the educated Catholic clergy throughout the world.

The subject of slavery, and the condition and prospects of the Negro race in Cuba, the probable results of the coolie system, and the relations between Church and State in Cuba, and the manner in which Sunday is treated in Havana, the public school system in America, the fate of Mormonism, and how our government will treat it, were freely discussed. It is not because I have any reason to suppose that these gentlemen would object to all they said being printed in these pages, and read by all who may choose to read it in Cuba, or the United States, that I do not report their interesting and instructive conversation; but because it would be, in my opinion, a violation of the universal understanding among gentlemen.

After dinner, we walked on the piazza, with the noble sunset view of the unsurpassed panorama lying before us; and I took my leave of my host, a kind and courteous gentleman of Old Spain, as well as a prelate, just as a few lights were beginning to sprinkle over the fading city, and the Morro Light to gleam on the untroubled air.

Made two visits in the city this evening. In each house, I found the double row of chairs, facing each other, always with about four or five feet of space between the rows. The etiquette is that the gentlemen sit on the row opposite to the ladies, if there be but two or three present. If a lady, on entering goes to the side of a gentleman, when the other row is open to her, it indicates either familiar acquaintance or boldness. There is no people so observant of outguards, as the Spanish race.

I notice, and my observation is supported by what I am told by the residents here, that there is no street-walking, in the technical sense, in Havana. Whether this is from the fact that no ladies walk in the streets—which are too narrow for comfortable or even safe walking—or by reason of police regulations, I do not know. From what one meets with in the streets, if he does not look farther, one would not know that there was a vice in Havana, not even drunkenness.

VII

HAVANA: Belén and the Jesuits

Rose before six, and walked as usual, down the Paseo, to the sea baths. How refreshing is this bath, after the hot night and close rooms! At your side, the wide blue sea with its distant sails, the bath cut into the clean rock, the gentle washing in and out of the tideless sea, at the Gulf Stream temperature, in the cool of the morning! As I pass down, I meet a file of coolies, in Chinese costume, marching, under overseers, to their work or their jail. And there is the chain-gang! clank, clank, as they go headed by officers with pistols and swords, and flanked by drivers with whips. This is simple wretchedness!

While at breakfast, a gentleman in the dress of the regular clergy, speaking English, called upon me, bringing me, from the bishop an open letter of introduction and admission to all the religious, charitable, and educational institutions of the city, and offering to conduct me to the Belén (Bethlehem). He is Father B. of Charleston, S. C. temporarily in Havana, with whom I find I have some acquaintances in common, both in America and abroad. We drive together to the Belén. I say drive; for few persons walk far in Havana, after ten o'clock in the morning. The volantes are the public carriages of Havana; and are as abundant as cabs in London. You never need stand long at a street door without finding one. The postilions are always Negroes; and I am told that they pay the owner a certain sum per day for the horse and volante, and make what they can above that.

The Belén is a group of buildings, of the usual yellow or tawny color, covering a good deal of ground, and of a thoroughly monastic character. It was first a Franciscan monastery, then a barrack, and now has been given by the government to the Jesuits. The company of Jesus here is composed of a rector and about forty clerical and twenty lay brethren. These perform every office, from the highest scientific investigations and instruction, down to the lowest menial offices, in the care of the children; some serving in costly vestments at the high altar, and others in coarse black garb at the gates. It is only three years since they established themselves in Havana, but in that time they have formed a school of two hundred boarders and one hundred day scholars, built dormitories for the boarders, and a common hall, restored the church and made it the most fully attended in the city; established a missionary work in all parts of the town, recalled a great number to the discipline of the Church, and not only created something like an enthusiasm of devotion among the women, who are said to have monopolized the religion of Cuba in times past, but have introduced among the men, and among many influential men, the practices of confession and communion, to which they had been almost entirely strangers. I do not take this account from the Jesuits themselves, but from the regular clergy of other orders, and from Protestants who are opposed to them and their influence. All agree that they are at work with zeal and success.

I met my distinguished acquaintance of yesterday, the rector, who took me to the boys' chapel, and introduced me to Father Antonio Cabre, a very young man of a spare frame and intellectual countenance, with hands so white and so thin, and eyes so bright, and cheek so pale! He is at the head of the department of mathematics and astronomy, and looks indeed as if he had outwatched the stars, in vigils of science or of devotion. He took me to his laboratory, his observatory, and his apparatus of philosophic instruments. These I am told are according to the latest inventions, and in the best style of French and German workmanship. I was also shown a collection of coins and medals, a cabinet of shells, the commencement of a museum of natural history, already enriched with most of the birds of Cuba, and an interesting cabinet of the woods of the island, in small blocks, each piece being polished on one side, and rough on the other. Among the woods were the mahoganies, the iron-wood, the ebony, the lignum vitæ, the cedar, and many others, of names unfamiliar to me, which admit of the most exquisite polish. Some of the most curious were from the Isla de Pinos, an island belonging to Cuba, and on its southern shore.

The sleeping arrangement for the boys here seemed to me to be new, and to be well adapted to the climate. There is a large hall, with a roof about thirty feet from the floor, and windows near the top, to give light and ventilation above, and small portholes, near the ground, to let air into the passages. In this hall are double rows of compartments, like high pews, or, more profanely, like the large boxes in restaurants and chop-houses, open at the top, with curtains instead of doors, and each large enough to contain a single bed, a chair, and a toilet table. This ensures both privacy and the light and air of the great hall. The bedsteads are of iron; and nothing can exceed the neatness and order of the apartments. The boys' clothes are kept in another part of the house, and they take to their dormitories only the clothes that they are using. Each boy sleeps alone. Several of the Fathers sleep in the hall, in curtained rooms at the ends of the passage-ways, and a watchman walks the rounds all night, to guard against fire, and to give notice of sickness.

The boys have a playground, a gymnasium, and a riding-school. But although they like riding and fencing, they do not take to the robust exercises and sports of English schoolboys. An American whom I met here, who had spent several months at the school, told me that in their recreations they were more like girls, and like to sit a good deal, playing or working with their hands. He pointed out to me a boy, the son of an American mother, a lady to whom I brought letters and kind wishes from her many friends at the North, and told me that he had more pluck than any boy in the school.

The roof of the Belén is flat, and gives a pleasant promenade, in the open air, after the sun is gone down, which is much needed, as the buildings are in the dense part of the city.

The brethren of this order wear short hair, with the tonsure, and dress in coarse cassocks of plain black, coming to the feet, and buttoned close to the neck, with a cape, but with no white of collar above; and in these, they sweep like black spectres, about the passage-ways, and across the halls and court-yards. There are so many of them that they are able to give thorough and minute attention to the boys, not only in instruction, both secular and religious, but in their entire training and development.

From the scholastic part of the institution, I passed to the church. It is not very large, has an open marble floor, a gallery newly erected for the use of the brethren and other men, a sumptuous high altar, a sacristy and vestry behind, and a small altar, by which burned the undying lamp, indicating the presence of the Sacrament. In the vestry, I was shown the vestments for the service of the high altar, some of which are costly and gorgeous in the extreme, not probably exceeded by those of the Temple at Jerusalem in the palmiest days of the Jewish hierarchy. All are presents from wealthy devotees. One, an alb, had a circle of precious stones; and the lace alone on another, a present from a lady of rank, is said to have cost three thousand dollars. Whatever may be thought of the rightfulness of this expenditure, turning upon the old question as to which the alabaster box of ointment and the ordained costliness of the Jewish ritual "must give us pause," it cannot be said of the Jesuits that they live in cedar, while the ark of God rests in curtains; for the actual life of the streets hardly presents any greater contrast, than that between the sumptuousness of their apparel at the altar, and the coarseness and cheapness of their ordinary dress, the bareness of their rooms, and the apparent severity of their life.

The Cubans have a childish taste for excessive decoration. Their altars look like toyshops. A priest, not a Cuban, told me that he went to the high altar of the cathedral once, on a Christmas day, to officiate, and when his eye fell on the childish and almost profane attempts at symbolism—a kind of doll millinery, if he had not got so far that he could not retire without scandal, he would have left the duties of the day to others. At the Belén there is less of this; but the Jesuits find or think it necessary to conform a good deal to the popular taste.

In the sacristy, near the side altar, is a distressing image of the Virgin, not in youth, but the mother of the mature man, with a sword pierced through her heart—referring to the figurative prediction "a sword shall pierce through thine own soul also." The handle and a part of the blade remain without, while the marks of the deep wound are seen, and the countenance expresses the sorest agony of mind and body. It is painful, and beyond all legitimate scope of art, and haunts one, like a vision of actual misery. It is almost the only thing in the church of which I have brought away a distinct image in my memory.

A strange, eventful history is that of the Society of Jesus! Ignatius Loyola, a soldier and noble of Spain, renouncing arms and knighthood, hangs his trophies of war upon the altar of Monserrate. After intense studies and barefoot pilgrimages, persecuted by religious orders whose excesses he sought to restrain, and frowned upon by the Inquisition, he organizes, with Xavier and Faber, at Montmartre, a society of three. From this small beginning, spreading upwards and outwards, it overshadows the earth. Now, at the top of success, it is supposed to control half Christendom. Now, his order proscribed by State and Church alike and suppressed by the Pope himself, there is not a spot of earth in Catholic Christendom where the Jesuit can place the sole of his foot. In this hour of distress, he finds refuge in Russia, and in Protestant Prussia. Then, restored and tolerated, the order revives here and there in Europe, with a fitful life; and, at length, blazes out into a glory of missionary triumphs and martyrdoms in China, in India, in Africa, and in North America; and now, in these later days, we see it advancing everywhere to a new epoch of labor and influence. Thorough in education, perfect in discipline, absolute in obedience—as yielding, as indestructible, as all-pervading as water or as air!

The Jesuits make strong friends and strong enemies. Many, who are neither the one nor the other, say of them that their ethics are artificial, and their system unnatural; that they do not reform nature, but destroy it; that, aiming to use the world without abusing it, they reduce it to subjection and tutelage; that they are always either in dangerous power, or in disgrace; and although they may labor with more enthusiasm and self-consecration than any other order, and meet with astonishing successes for a time, yet such is the character of their system that these successes are never permanent, but result in opposition, not only from Protestants, and moderate Catholics, and from the civil power, but from other religious orders and from the regular clergy in their own Church, an opposition to which they are invariably compelled to yield, at last. In fine, they declare, that, allowing them all zeal, and all ability, and all devotedness, their system is too severe and too unnatural for permanent usefulness anywhere—medicine and not food, lightning and not light, flame and not warmth.

Not satisfied with this moderated judgment, their opponents have met them, always and everywhere, with uniform and vehement reprobation. They say to them—the opinion of mankind has condemned you! The just and irreversible sentence of time has made you a by-word and a hissing, and reduced your very name, the most sacred in its origin, to a synonym for ambition and deceit!

Others, again, esteem them the nearest approach in modern times to that type of men portrayed by one of the chiefest, in his epistle: "In much patience, in afflictions, in necessities, in distresses, in stripes, in imprisonments, in tumults, in labors, in watchings, in fastings; by pureness, by knowledge, by long-suffering; ... by honor and dishonor; by evil report and good report; as deceivers and yet true; as unknown, and yet well known; as dying, and behold we live; as chastened, and not killed; as sorrowful, and yet always rejoicing; as poor, yet making many rich; as having nothing, and yet possessing all things."

VIII

MATANZAS

As there are no plantations to be seen near Havana, I determine to go down to Matanzas, near which the sugar plantations are in full tide of operation at this season. A steamer leaves here every night at ten o'clock, reaching Matanzas before daylight, the distance by sea being between fifty and sixty miles.

Took this steamer to-night. She got under way punctually at ten o'clock, and steamed down the harbor. The dark waters are alive with phosphorescent light. From each ship that lies moored, the cable from the bows, tautened to its anchor, makes a run of silver light. Each boat, gliding silently from ship to ship, and shore to shore, turns up a silver ripple at its stem, and trails a wake of silver behind; while the dip of the oar-blades brings up liquid silver, dripping, from the opaque deep. We pass along the side of the two-decker, and see through her ports the lanterns and men; under the stern of one frigate, and across the bows of another (for Havana is well supplied with men-of-war); and drop leisurely down by the Cabaña, where we are hailed from the rocks; and bend round the Morro, and are out on the salt, rolling sea. Having a day of work before me, I went early to my berth, and was waked up by the letting off of steam, in the lower harbor of Matanzas, at three o'clock in the morning. My fellow-passengers, who sat up, said the little steamer tore and plunged, and jumped through the water like a thing that had lost its wits. They seemed to think that the Cuban engineer had got a machine that would some day run away with him. It was, certainly, a very short passage.

We passed a good many vessels lying at anchor in the lower harbor of Matanzas, and came to anchor about a mile from the pier. It was clear, bright moonlight. The small boats came off to us, and took us and our luggage ashore. I was landed alone on a quay, carpet-bag in hand, and had to guess my way to the inn, which was near the water-side. I beat on the big, close-barred door; and a sleepy Negro, in time, opened it. Mine host was up, expecting passengers, and after waiting on the very tardy movements of the Negro, who made a separate journey to the yard for each thing the room needed, I got to bed by four o'clock, on the usual piece of canvas stretched over an iron frame, in a room having a brick floor, and windows without glass closed with big-bolted shutters.

After coffee, walked out to deliver my letters to Mr.——, an American merchant, who has married the daughter of a planter, a gentleman of wealth and character. He is much more agreeable and painstaking than we have any right to expect of one who is served so frequently with notice that his attentions are desired for the entertainment of a stranger. Knowing that it is my wish to visit a plantation, he gives me a letter to Don Juan Chartrand, who has an ingenio (sugar plantation), called La Ariadne, near Limonar, and about twenty-five miles back in the country from Matanzas. The train leaves at 2.30 P.M., which gives me several hours for the city.

Although it is not yet nine o'clock, it is very hot, and one is glad to keep on the shady side of the broad streets of Matanzas. This city was built later and more under foreign direction than Havana, and I have been told, not by persons here however, that for many years the controlling influences of society were French, English, and American; but that lately the policy of the government has been to discourage foreign influence, and now Spanish customs prevail—bull-fights have been introduced, and other usages and entertainments which had had no place here before. Whatever may be the reason, this city differs from Havana in buildings, vehicles, and dress, and in the width of its streets, and has less of the peculiar air of a tropical city. It has about 25,000 inhabitants, and stands where two small rivers, the Yumurí and the San Juan, crossed by handsome stone bridges, run into the sea, dividing the city into three parts. The vessels lie at anchor from one to three miles below the city, and lighters, with masts and sails, line the stone quays of the little rivers. The city is flat and hot, but the country around is picturesque, hilly, and fertile. To the westward of the town, rises a ridge, bordering on the sea, called the Cumbre, which is a place of resort for the beauty of its views; and in front of the Cumbre, on the inland side, is the deep rich valley of the Yumurí, with its celebrated cavern. These I must see, if I can, on my return from the plantation.

In my morning walk, I see a company of coolies, in the hot sun, carrying stones to build a house, under the eye of a taskmaster who sits in the shade. The stones have been dropped in a pile, from carts, and the coolies, carry them, in files, to the cellar of the house. They are naked to the waist, with short-legged cotton trousers coming to the knees. Some of these men were strongly, one or two of them powerfully built, but many seemed very thin and frail. While looking on, I saw an evident American face near me, and getting into conversation with the man, found him an intelligent shipmaster from New York, who had lived in Matanzas for a year or two, engaged in business. He told me, as I had heard in Havana, that the importer of the coolies gets $400 a head for them from the purchaser, and that the coolies are entitled from the purchaser to four dollars a month, which they may demand monthly if they choose, and are bound to eight years' service, during which time they may be held to all the service that a slave is subject to. They are more intelligent, and are put to higher labor than the Negro. He said, too, it would not do to flog a coolie. Idolaters as they are, they have a notion of the dignity of the human body, at least as against strangers, which does not allow them to submit to the indignity of corporal chastisement. If a coolie is flogged, somebody must die; either the coolie himself, for they are fearfully given to suicide, or the perpetrator of the indignity, or some one else, according to their strange principles of vicarious punishment. Yet such is the value of labor in Cuba, that a citizen will give $400, in cash, for the chance of enforcing eight years' labor, at $4 per month, from a man speaking a strange language, worshipping strange gods or none, thinking suicide a virtue, and governed by no moral laws in common with his master—his value being yet further diminished by the chances of natural death, of sickness, accident, escape, and of forfeiting his services to the government, for any crime he may commit against laws he does not understand.

The Plaza is in the usual style—an enclosed garden, with walks; and in front is the Government House. In this spot, so fair and so still in the noonday sun, some fourteen years ago, under the fire of the platoons of Spanish soldiers, fell the patriot and poet, one of the few popular poets of Cuba, Gabriel de la Concepción Valdez. Charged with being the head of that concerted movement of the slaves for their freedom which struck such terror into Cuba, in 1844, he was convicted and ordered to be shot. At the first volley, as the story is told, he was only wounded. "Aim here!" said he, pointing to his head. Another volley, and it was all over.

The name and story of Gabriel de la Concepción Valdez are preserved by the historians and tourists of Cuba. He is best known, however, by the name of Placido, that under which he wrote and published, than by his proper name. He was a man of genius and a man of valor, but—he was a mulatto!

IX

TO LIMONAR BY TRAIN

Took the train for Limonar, at 2.30 P.M. There are three classes of cars, all after the American model, the first of about the condition of our first-class cars when on the point of being condemned as worn out; the second, a little plainer; and the third, only covered wagons with benches. The car I entered had "Davenport & Co., makers, Cambridgeport, Mass.," familiarly on its front, and the next had "Eaton, Gilbert & Co., Troy, N. York." The brakemen on the train are coolies, one of them a handsome lad, with coarse, black hair, that lay gracefully about his head, and eyes handsome, though of the Chinese pattern. They were all dressed in the common shirt, trousers and hat, and, but for their eyes, might be taken for men of any of the Oriental races.

As we leave Matanzas, we rise on an ascending grade, and the bay and city lie open before us. The bay is deep on the western shore, under the ridge of the Cumbre, and there the vessels lie at anchor; while the rest of the bay is shallow, and its water, in this state of the sky and light, is of a pale green color. The lighters, with sail and oar are plying between the quays and the vessels below. All is pretty and quiet and warm, but the scene has none of those regal points that so impress themselves on the imagination and memory in the surroundings of Havana.

I am now to get my first view of the interior of Cuba. I could not have a more favorable day. The air is clear, and not excessively hot. The soft clouds float midway in the serene sky, the sun shines fair and bright, and the luxuriance of a perpetual summer covers the face of nature. These strange palm trees everywhere! I cannot yet feel at home among them. Many of the other trees are like our own, and though, tropical in fact, look to the eye as if they might grow as well in New England as here. But the royal palm looks so intensely and exclusively tropical! It cannot grow beyond this narrow belt of the earth's surface. Its long, thin body, so straight and so smooth, swathed from the foot—in a tight bandage of tawny gray, leaving only its deep-green neck, and over that its crest and plumage of deep-green leaves! It gives no shade, and bears no fruit that is valued by men. And it has no beauty to atone for those wants. Yet it has more than beauty—a strange fascination over the eye and the fancy, that will never allow it to be overlooked or forgotten. The palm tree seems a kind of *lusus naturae* to the northern eye—an exotic wherever you meet it. It seems to be conscious of its want of usefulness for food or shade, yet has a dignity of its own, a pride of unmixed blood and royal descent—the hidalgo of the soil.

What are those groves and clusters of small growth, looking like Indian corn in a state of transmigration into trees, the stalk turning into a trunk, a thin soft coating half changed to bark, and the ears of corn turning into melons? Those are the bananas and plantains, as their bunches of green and yellow fruits plainly enough indicate, when you come nearer. But, that sad, weeping tree, its long yellow-green leaves drooping to the ground! What can that be? It has a green fruit like a melon. There it is again, in groves! I interrupt my neighbor's tenth cigarrito, to ask him the name of the tree. It is the cocoa! And that soft green melon becomes the hard shell we break with a hammer. Other trees there are, in abundance, of various forms and foliage, but they might have grown in New England or New York, so far as the eye can teach us; but the palm, the cocoa, the banana and plantain are the characteristic trees you could not possibly meet with in any other zone.

Thickets—jungles I might call them—abound. It seems as if a bird could hardly get through them; yet they are rich with wild flowers of all forms and colors, the white, the purple, the pink, and the blue. The trees are full of birds of all plumage. There is one like our brilliant oriole. I cannot hear their notes, for the clatter of the train. Stone fences, neatly laid up, run across the lands;— not of our cold bluish-gray granite, the color, as a friend once said, of a miser's eye, but of soft, warm brown and russet, and well overgrown with creepers, and fringed with flowers. There are avenues, and here are clumps of the prim orange tree, with its dense and deep-green polished foliage gleaming with golden fruit. Now we come to acres upon acres of the sugar-cane, looking at a distance like fields of overgrown broomcorn. It grows to the height of eight or ten feet, and very thick. An army could be hidden in it. This soil must be deeply and intensely fertile.

There, at the end of an avenue of palms, in a nest of shade-trees, is a group of white buildings, with a sea of cane-fields about it, with one high furnace-chimney, pouring out its volume of black smoke. This is a sugar plantation— my first sight of an ingenio; and the chimney is for the steam works of the sugar-house. It is the height of the sugar season, and the untiring engine toils and smokes day and night. Ox carts, loaded with cane, are moving slowly to the sugar-house from the fields; and about the house, and in the fields, in various attitudes and motions of labor, are the Negroes, men and women and children, some cutting the cane, some loading the carts, and some tending the mill and the furnace. It is a busy scene of distant industry, in the afternoon sun of a languid Cuban day.

Now these groups of white one-story buildings become more frequent, sometimes very near each other, all having the same character—the group of white buildings, the mill, with its tall furnace-chimney, and the look of a distillery, and all differing from each other only in the number and extent of the buildings, or in the ornament and comfort of shade-trees and avenues about them. Some are approached by broad alleys of the palm, or mango, or orange, and have gardens around them, and stand under clusters of shade-trees; while others glitter in the hot sun, on the flat sea of cane-fields, with only a little oasis of shade-trees and fruit-trees immediately about the houses.

I now begin to feel that I am in Cuba; in the tropical, rich, sugar-growing, slave-tilled Cuba. Heretofore, I have seen only the cities and their environs in which there are more things that are common to the rest of the world. The country life tells the story of any people that have a country life. The New England farm-house shows the heart of New England. The mansion-house and cottage show the heart of Old England. The plantation life that I am seeing and about to see, tells the story of Cuba, the Cuba that has been and that is.

As we stop at one station, which seems to be in the middle of a cane-field, the Negroes and coolies go to the cane, slash off a piece with their knives, cut off the rind and chew the stick of soft, saccharine pulp, the juice running out of their mouths as they eat. They seem to enjoy it so highly, that I am tempted to try the taste of it, myself. But I shall have time for all this at La Ariadne.

These stations consist merely of one or two buildings, where the produce of the neighborhood is collected for transportation, and at which there are very few passengers. The railroad is intended for the carriage of sugar and other produce, and gets its support almost entirely in that way; for it runs through a sparse, rural population, where there are no towns; yet so large and valuable is the sugar crop that I believe the road is well supported. At each station are its hangers-on of free Negroes, a few slaves on duty as carriers, a few low whites, and now and then someone who looks as if he might be an overseer or mayoral of a plantation.

Limonar appears in large letters on the small building where we next stop, and I get out and inquire of a squad of idlers for the plantation of Señor Chartrand. They point to a group of white buildings about a quarter of a mile distant, standing prettily under high shade-trees, and approached by an avenue of orange trees. Getting a tall Negro to shoulder my bag, for a real, I walk to the house. It is an afternoon of exquisite beauty. How can any one have a weather sensation, in such an air as this? There is no current of the slightest chill anywhere, neither is it oppressively hot. The air is serene and pure and light. The sky gives its mild assurance of settled fair weather. All about me is rich verdure, over a gently undulating surface of deeply fertile country, with here and there a high hill in the horizon, and, on one side, a ridge that may be called mountains. There is no sound but that of the birds, and in the next tree they may be counted by hundreds. Wild flowers, of all colors and scents, cover the ground and the thickets. This is the famous red earth, too. The avenue looks as if it had been laid down with pulverized brick, and all the dust on any object you see is red. Now we turn into the straight avenue of orange trees—prim, deep green trees, glittering with golden fruit. Here is the one-story, high-roofed house, with long, high piazzas. There is a high wall, carefully whitewashed, enclosing a square with one gate, looking like a garrisoned spot. That must be the Negroes' quarters; for there is a group of little Negroes at the gate, looking earnestly at the approaching stranger. Beyond is the sugar-house, and the smoking chimney, and the ox carts, and the field hands. Through the wide, open door of the mansion, I see two gentlemen at dinner, an older and a younger—the head of gray, and the head of black, and two Negro women, one serving, and the other swinging her brush to disperse the flies. Two big, deep-mouthed hounds come out and bark; and the younger gentleman looks at us, comes out, and calls off the dogs. My Negro stops at the path and touches his hat, waiting permission to go to the piazza with the luggage; for Negroes do not go to the house door without previous leave, in strictly ordered plantations. I deliver my letter, and in a moment am received with such cordial welcome that I am made to feel as if I had conferred a favor by coming to see them.

X

A SUGAR PLANTATION: The Labor

At some seasons, a visit may be a favor, on remote plantations; but I know this is the height of the sugar season, when every hour is precious to the master. After a brief toilet, I sit down with them; for they have just begun dinner. In five minutes, I am led to feel as if I were a friend of many years. Both gentlemen speak English like a native tongue. To the younger it is so, for he was born in South Carolina, and his mother is a lady of that state. The family are not here. They do not live on the plantation, but in Matanzas. The plantation is managed by the son, who resides upon it; the father coming out occasionally for a few days, as now, in the busy season.

The dinner is in the Spanish style, which I am getting attached to. I should flee from a joint, or a sirloin. We have rice, excellently cooked, as always in Cuba, eggs with it, if we choose, and fried plantains, sweet potatoes, mixed dishes of fowl and vegetables, with a good deal of oil and seasoning, in which a hot red pepper, about the size of the barberry, prevails. Catalonia wine, which is pretty sure to be pure, is their table claret, while sherry, which also comes direct from the mother-country, is for dessert. I have taken them by surprise, in the midst of the busiest season, in a house where there are no ladies; yet the table, the service, the dress and the etiquette, are none the less in the style of good society. There seems to be no letting down, where letting down would be so natural and excusable.

I suppose the fact that the land and the agricultural capital of the interior are in the hands of an upper class, which does no manual labor, and which has enough of wealth and leisure to secure the advantages of continued intercourse with city and foreign society, and of occasional foreign travel, tends to preserve throughout the remote agricultural districts, habits and tone and etiquette, which otherwise would die out, in the entire absence of large towns and of high local influences.

Whoever has met with a book called "Evenings in Boston," and read the story of the old Negro, Saturday, and seen the frontispiece of the Negro fleeing through the woods of Santo Domingo, with two little white boys, one in each hand, will know as much of Mr. Chartrand, the elder, as I did the day before seeing him. He is the living hero, or rather subject, for Saturday was the hero, of that tale. His father was a wealthy planter of Santo Domingo, a Frenchman, of large estates, with wife, children, friends and neighbors. These were gathered about him in a social circle in his house, when the dreadful insurrection overtook them, and father, mother, sons, and daughters were murdered in one night, and only two of the children, boys of eight and ten, were saved by the fidelity of Saturday, an old and devoted house servant.

Saturday concealed the boys, got them off the island, took them to Charleston, South Carolina, where they found friends among the Huguenot families, and the refugees from Santo Domingo. There Mr. Chartrand grew up; and after a checkered and adventurous early life, a large part of it on the sea, he married a lady of worth and culture, in South Carolina, and settled himself as a planter, on this spot, nearly forty years ago. His plantation he named "El Laberinto," (The Labyrinth,) after a favorite vessel he had commanded, and for thirty years it was a prosperous cafetal, the home of a happy family, and much visited by strangers from. America and Europe. The causes which broke up the coffee estates of Cuba carried this with the others; and it was converted into a sugar plantation, under the new name of La Ariadne, from the fancy of Ariadne having shown the way out of the Labyrinth. Like most of the sugar estates, it is no longer the regular home of its proprietors.

The change from coffee plantations to sugar plantations—from the cafetal to the ingenio, has seriously affected the social, as it has the economic condition of Cuba.

Coffee must grow under shade. Consequently the coffee estate was, in the first place, a plantation of trees, and by the hundred acres. Economy and taste led the planters, who were chiefly the French refugees from Santo Domingo to select fruit trees, and trees valuable for their wood, as well as pleasing for their beauty and shade. Under these plantations of trees, grew the coffee plant, an evergreen, and almost an ever-flowering plant, with berries of changing hues, and, twice a year, brought its fruit to maturity. That the coffee might be tended and gathered, avenues wide enough for wagons must be carried through the plantations, at frequent intervals. The plantation was, therefore, laid out like a garden, with avenues and foot-paths, all under the shade of the finest trees, and the spaces between the avenues were groves of fruit trees and shade trees, under which grew, trimmed down to the height of five or six feet, the coffee plant. The labor of the plantation was in tending, picking, drying, and shelling the coffee, and gathering the fresh fruits of trees for use and for the market, and for preserves and sweetmeats, and in raising vegetables and poultry, and rearing sheep and horned cattle and horses. It was a beautiful and simple horticulture, on a very large scale. Time was required to perfect this garden—the Cubans call it paradise—of a cafetal; but when matured, it was a cherished home. It required and admitted of no extraordinary mechanical power, or of the application of steam, or of science, beyond the knowledge of soils, of simple culture, and of plants and trees.

For twenty years and more it has been forced upon the knowledge of the reluctant Cubans, that Brazil, the West India islands to the southward of Cuba, and the Spanish Main, can excel them in coffee-raising. The successive disastrous hurricanes of 1843 and 1845, which destroyed many and damaged most of the coffee estates, added to the colonial system of the mother-country, which did not give extraordinary protection to this product, are commonly said to have put an end to the coffee plantations. Probably, they only hastened a change which must at some time have come. But the same causes of soil and climate which made Cuba inferior in coffee-growing, gave her a marked superiority in the cultivation of sugar. The damaged plantations were not restored as coffee estates, but were laid down to the sugar-cane; and gradually, first in the western and northern parts, and daily extending easterly and southerly over the entire island, the exquisite cafetals have been prostrated and dismantled, the groves of shade and fruit trees cut down, the avenues and foot-paths ploughed up, and the denuded land laid down to wastes of sugar-cane.

The sugar-cane allows of no shade. Therefore the groves and avenues must fall. To make its culture profitable, it must be raised in the largest possible quantities that the extent of land will permit. To attempt the raising of fruit, or of the ornamental woods, is bad economy for the sugar planter. Most of the fruits, especially the orange, which is the chief export, ripen in the midst of the sugar season, and no hands can be spared to attend to them. The sugar planter often buys the fruits he needs for daily use and for making preserves, from the neighboring cafetals. The cane ripens but once a year. Between the time when enough of it is ripe to justify beginning to work the mill, and the time when the heat and rains spoil its qualities, all the sugar-making of the year must be done. In Louisiana, this period does not exceed eight weeks. In Cuba it is full four months. This gives Cuba a great advantage. Yet these four months are short enough; and during that time, the steam-engine plies and the furnace fires burn night and day.

Sugar-making brings with it steam, fire, smoke, and a drive of labor, and admits of and requires the application of science. Managed with skill and energy, it is extremely productive. Indifferently managed, it may be a loss. The sugar estate is not valuable, like the coffee estate, for what the land will produce, aided by ordinary and quiet manual labor only. Its value is in the skill, and the character of the labor. The land is there, and the Negroes are there; but the result is loss or gain, according to the amount of labor that can be obtained, and the skill with which the manual labor and the mechanical powers are applied. It is said that at the present time, in the present state of the market, a well-managed sugar estate yields from fifteen to twenty-five per cent on the investment. This is true, I am inclined to think, if by the investment be meant only the land, the machinery, and the slaves. But the land is not a large element in the investment. The machinery is costly, yet its value depends on the science applied to its construction and operation. The chief item in the investment is the slave labor. Taking all the slaves together, men, women, and children, the young and the old, the sick and the well, the good and the bad, their market value averages about $1000 a head. Yet of these, allowing for those too young or too old, for the sick, and for those who must tend the young, the old and the sick, and for those whose labor, like that of the cooks, only sustains the others, not more than one half are able-bodied, productive laborers. The value of this chief item in the investment depends largely on moral and intellectual considerations. How unsatisfactory is it, then, to calculate the profits of the investment, when you leave out of the calculation the value of the controlling power, the power that extorts the contributions of labor from the steam and the engine and the fire, and from the more difficult human will. This is the "plus x" of the formula, which, unascertained, gives us little light as to the result.

But, to return to the changes wrought by this substitution of sugar for coffee. The sugar plantation is no grove, or garden, or orchard. It is not the home of the pride and affections of the planter's family. It is not a coveted, indeed, hardly a desirable residence. Such families as would like to remain on these plantations are driven off for want of neighboring society. Thus the estates, largely abandoned by the families of the planters, suffer the evils of absenteeism, while the owners live in the suburbs of Havana and Matanzas, and in the Fifth Avenue of New York. The slave system loses its patriarchal character. The master is not the head of a great family, its judge, its governor, its physician, its priest and its father, as the fond dream of the advocates of slavery, and sometimes, doubtless, the reality, made him. Middlemen, in the shape of administradores, stand between the owner and the slaves. The slave is little else than an item of labor raised or bought. The sympathies of common home, common childhood, long and intimate relations and many kind offices, common attachments to house, to land, to dogs, to cattle, to trees, to birds—the knowledge of births, sicknesses, and deaths, and the duties and sympathies of a common religion—all those things that may ameliorate the legal relations of the master and slave, and often give to the face of servitude itself precarious but interesting features of beauty and strength—these they must not look to have. This change has had some effect already, and will produce much more, on the social system of Cuba.

There are still plantations on which the families of the wealthy and educated planters reside. And in some cases the administrador is a younger member or a relative of the family, holding the same social position; and the permanent administrador will have his family with him. Yet, it is enough to say that the same causes which render the ingenio no longer a desirable residence for the owner make it probable that the administrador will be either a dependent or an adventurer; a person from whom the owner will expect a great deal, and the slaves but little, and from whom none will get all they expect, and perhaps none all they are entitled to.

In the afternoon we went to the sugar-house, and I was initiated into the mysteries of the work. There are four agents: steam, fire, cane juice, and Negroes. The results are sugar and molasses. At this ingenio, they make only the Muscovado, or brown sugar. The processes are easily described, but it is difficult to give an idea of the scene. It is one of condensed and determined labor.

To begin at the beginning, the cane is cut from the fields by companies of men and women, working together, who use an instrument called a machete, which is something between a sword and a cleaver. Two blows with this slash off the long leaves, and a third blow cuts off the stalk, near to the ground. At this work, the laborers move like reapers, in even lines, at stated distances. Before them is a field of dense, high-waving cane; and behind them, strewn wrecks of stalks and leaves. Near, and in charge of the party, stands a driver, or more grandiloquently, a contramayoral, with the short, limber plantation whip, the badge of his office, under his arm.

Ox-carts pass over the field, and are loaded with the cane, which they carry to the mill. The oxen are worked in the Spanish fashion, the yoke being strapped upon the head, close to the horns, instead of being hung round the neck, as with us, and are guided by goads, and by a rope attached to a ring through the nostrils. At the mill, the cane is tipped from the carts into large piles, by the side of the platform. From these piles, it is placed carefully, by hand, lengthwise, in a long trough. This trough is made of slats, and moved by the power of the endless chain, connected with the engine. In this trough, it is carried between heavy, horizontal, cylindrical rollers, where it is crushed, its juice falling into receivers below, and the crushed cane passing off and falling into a pile on the other side.

This crushed cane (bagazo), falling from between the rollers, is gathered into baskets by men and women, who carry it on their heads into the fields and spread it for drying. There it is watched and tended as carefully as new-mown grass in haymaking, and raked into cocks or windrows, on an alarm of rain. When dry, it is placed under sheds for protection against wet. From the sheds and from the fields, it is loaded into carts and drawn to the furnace doors, into which it is thrown by Negroes, who crowd it in by the armful, and rake it about with long poles. Here it feeds the perpetual fires by which the steam is made, the machinery moved, and the cane-juice boiled. The care of the bagazo is an important part of the system; for if that becomes wet and fails, the fires must stop, or resort be had to wood, which is scarce and expensive.

Thus, on one side of the rollers is the ceaseless current of fresh, full, juicy cane-stalks, just cut from the open field; and on the other side, is the crushed, mangled, juiceless mass, drifting out at the draught, and fit only to be cast into the oven and burned. This is the way of the world, as it is the course of art. The cane is made to destroy itself. The ruined and corrupted furnish the fuel and fan the flame that lures on and draws in and crushes the fresh and wholesome; and the operation seems about as mechanical and unceasing in the one case as in the other.

From the rollers, the juice falls below into a large receiver, from which it flows into great, open vats, called defecators. These defecators are heated by the exhaust steam of the engine, led through them in pipes. All the steam condensed forms water, which is returned warm into the boiler of the engine. In the defecators, as their name denotes, the scum of the juice is purged off, so far as heat alone will do it. From the last defecator, the juice is passed through a trough into the first caldron. Of the caldrons, there is a series, or, as they call it, a train, through all which the juice must go. Each caldron is a large, deep, copper vat, heated very hot, in which the juice seethes and boils. At each, stands a strong Negro, with long, heavy skimmer in hand, stirring the juice and skimming off the surface. This scum is collected and given to the hogs, or thrown upon the muck heap, and is said to be very fructifying. The juice is ladled from one caldron to the next, as fast as the office of each is finished. From the last caldron, where its complete crystallization is effected, it is transferred to coolers, which are large, shallow pans. When fully cooled, it looks like brown sugar and molasses mixed. It is then shovelled from the coolers into hogsheads. These hogsheads have holes bored in their bottoms; and, to facilitate the drainage, strips of cane are placed in the hogshead, with their ends in these holes, and the hogs-head is filled. The hogsheads are set on open frames, under which are copper receivers, on an inclined plane, to catch and carry off the drippings from the hogsheads. These drippings are the molasses, which is collected and put into tight casks.

I believe I have given the entire process. When it is remembered that all this, in every stage, is going on at once, within the limits of the mill, it may well be supposed to present a busy scene. The smell of juice and of sugar-vapor, in all its stages, is intense. The Negroes fatten on it. The clank of the engine, the steady grind of the machines, and the high, wild cry of the Negroes at the caldrons to the stokers at the furnace doors, as they chant out their directions or wants—now for more fire, and now to scatter the fire—which must be heard above the din, "A-a-b'la! A-a-b'la!" "E-e-cha candela!" "Pu-er-ta!", and the barbaric African chant and chorus of the gang at work filling the cane-troughs—all these make the first visit at the sugar-house a strange experience. But after one or two visits, the monotony is as tiresome as the first view is exciting. There is, literally, no change in the work. There are the same noises of the machines, the same cries from Negroes at the same spots, the same intensely sweet smell, the same state of the work in all its stages, at whatever hour you visit it, whether in the morning, or evening, at midnight, or at the dawn of the day. If you wake up at night, you hear the "A-a-b'la! A-a-b'la!"

"E-e-cha! E-e-cha!" of the caldron-men crying to the stokers, and the high, monotonous chant of the gangs filling the wagons or the trough, a short, improvisated stave, and then the chorus—not a tune, like the song of sailors at the tackle and falls, but a barbaric, tuneless intonation.

When I went into the sugar-house, I saw a man with an unmistakably New England face in charge of the engine, with that look of intelligence and independence so different from the intelligence and independence of all other persons.

"Is not that a New England man?"

"Yes," said Mr. Chartrand, "he is from Lowell; and the engine was built in Lowell."

When I found him at leisure, I made myself known to him, and he sat down on the brickwork of the furnace, and had a good unburdening of talk; for he had not seen any one from the United States for three months. He talked, like a true Yankee, of law and politics—the Lowell Bar and Mr. Butler, Mr. Abbott and Mr. Wentworth; of the Boston Bar and Mr. Choate; of Massachusetts politics and Governor Banks; and of national politics and the Thirty Millions Bill, and whether it would pass, and what if it did.

This engineer is one of a numerous class, whom the sugar culture brings annually to Cuba. They leave home in the autumn, engage themselves for the sugar season, put the machinery in order, work it for the four or five months of its operation, clean and put it in order for lying by, and return to the United States in the spring. They must be machinists, as well as engineers; for all the repairs and contrivances, so necessary in a remote place, fall upon them. Their skill is of great value, and while on the plantation their work is incessant, and they have no society or recreations whatever. The occupation, however, is healthful, their position independent, and their pay large. This engineer had been several years in Cuba, and I found him well informed, and, I think, impartial and independent. He tells me, which I had also heard in Havana, that this plantation is a favorable specimen, both for skill and humanity, and is managed on principles of science and justice, and yields a large return. On many plantations—on most, I suspect, from all I can learn—the Negroes, during the sugar season, are allowed but four hours sleep in the twenty-four, with one for dinner, and a half hour for breakfast, the night being divided into three watches, of four hours each, the laborers taking their turns. On this plantation, the laborers are in two watches, and divide the night equally between them, which gives them six hours for sleep. In the day, they have half an hour for breakfast and one hour for dinner. Here, too, the very young and the very old are excused from the sugar-house, and the nursing mothers have lighter duties and frequent intervals of rest. The women worked at cutting the cane, feeding the mill, carrying the bagazo in baskets, spreading and drying it, and filling the wagons; but not in the sugar-house itself, or at the furnace doors. I saw that no boys or girls were in the mill—none but full-grown persons. The very small children do absolutely nothing all day, and the older children tend the cattle and run errands. And the engineer tells me that in the long run this liberal system of treatment, as to hours and duties, yields a better return than a more stringent rule.

He thinks the crop this year, which has been a favorable one, will yield, in well-managed plantations a net interest of from fifteen to twenty-five per cent on the investment; making no allowance, of course, for the time and skill of the master. This will be a clear return to planters like Mr. Chartrand, who do not eat up their profits by interest on advances, and have no mortgages, and require no advances from the merchants.

But the risks of the investment are great. The cane-fields are liable to fires, and these spread with great rapidity, and are difficult to extinguish. Last year Mr. Chartrand lost $7,000 in a few hours by fire. In the cholera season he lost $12,000 in a few days by deaths among the Negroes.

According to the usual mode of calculation, I suppose the value of the investment of Mr. Chartrand to be between $125,000 and $150,000. On well-managed estates of this size, the expenses should not exceed $10,000. The gross receipts, in sugar and molasses, at a fair rate of the markets, cannot average less than between $35,000 and $40,000. This should leave a profit of between eighteen and twenty-two per cent. Still, the worth of an estimate depends on the principle on which the capital is appraised. The number of acres laid down to cane, on this plantation, is about three hundred. The whole number of Negroes is one hundred, and of these not more than half, at any time, are capable of efficient labor; and there are twenty-two children below the age of five years, out of a total of one hundred Negroes.

Beside the engineer, some large plantations have one or more white assistants; but here an intelligent Negro has been taught enough to take charge of the engine when the engineer is off duty. This is the highest post a Negro can reach in the mill, and this Negro was mightily pleased when I addressed him as maquinista. There are, also, two or three white men employed, during the season, as sugar masters. Their post is beside the caldrons and defecators, where they are to watch the work in all its stages, regulate the heat and the time for each removal, and oversee the men. These, with the engineer, make the force of white men who are employed for the season.

The regular and permanent officers of a plantation are the mayoral and mayordomo. The mayoral is, under the master or his administrador, the chief mate or first lieutenant of the ship. He has the general oversight of the Negroes, at their work or in their houses, and has the duty of exacting labor and enforcing discipline. Much depends on his character, as to the comfort of master and slaves. If he is faithful and just, there may be ease and comfort; but if he is not, the slaves are never sure of justice, and the master is sure of nothing. The mayoral comes, of necessity, from the middle class of whites, and is usually a native Cuban, and it is not often that a satisfactory one can be found or kept. The day before I arrived, in the height of the season, Mr. Chartrand had been obliged to dismiss his mayoral, on account of his conduct to the women, which was producing the worst results with them and with the men; and not long before, one was dismissed for conniving with the Negroes in a wholesale system of theft, of which he got the lion's share.

The mayordomo is the purser, and has the immediate charge of the stores, produce, materials for labor, and provisions for consumption, and keeps the accounts. On well regulated plantations, he is charged with all the articles of use or consumption, and with the products as soon as they are in condition to be numbered, weighed, or counted, and renders his accounts of what is consumed or destroyed, and of the produce sent away. There is also a boyero, who is the herdsman, and has charge of all the cattle. He is sometimes a Negro.

Under the mayoral, are a number of contramayorales, who are the boatswain's mates of the ship, and correspond to the "drivers" of our southern plantations. One of them goes with every gang when set to work, whether in the field or elsewhere, and whether men or women, and watches and directs them, and enforces labor from them. The drivers carry under the arm, at all times, the short, limber plantation whip, the badge of their office and their means of compulsion. They are almost always Negroes; and it is generally thought that Negroes are not more humane in this office than the low whites. On this plantation, it is three years since any slave has been whipped; and that punishment is never inflicted here on a woman. Near the Negro quarters, is a penitentiary, which is of stone, with three cells for solitary confinement, each dark, but well ventilated. Confinement in these, on bread and water, is the extreme punishment that has been found necessary for the last three years. The Negro fears solitude and darkness, and covets his food, fire, and companionship.

With all the corps of hired white labor, the master must still be the real power, and on his character the comfort and success of the plantation depend. If he has skill as a chemist, a geologist, or a machinist, it is not lost; but, except as to the engineer, who may usually be relied upon, the master must be capable of overseeing the whole economy of the plantation, or all will go wrong. His chief duty is to oversee the overseers, to watch his officers, the mayoral, the mayordomo, the boyero, and the sugar masters. These are mere hirelings, and of a low sort, such as a slave system reduces them to; and if they are lazy, the work slackens; and if they are ill-natured, somebody suffers. The mere personal presence of the master operates as a stimulus to the work. This afternoon young Mr. Chartrand and I took horses and rode out to the cane-field, where the people were cutting. They had been at work a half hour. He stopped his horse where they were when we came to them, and the next half hour, without a word from him, they had made double the distance of the first. It seems to me that the work of a plantation is what a clock would be that always required a man's hand pressing on the main spring. With the slave, the ultimate sanction is force. The motives of pride, shame, interest, ambition, and affection may be appealed to, and the minor punishments of degradation in duties, deprivation of food and sleep, and solitary confinement may be resorted to; but the whip, which the driver always carries, reminds the slave that if all else fails, the infliction of painful bodily punishment lies behind, and will be brought to bear, rather than that the question be left unsettled. Whether this extreme be reached, and how often it be reached, depends on the personal qualities of the master. If he is lacking in self-control, he will fall into violence. If he has not the faculty of ruling by moral and intellectual power—be he ever so humane, if he is not firm and intelligent, the bad among the slaves will get the upper hand; and he will be in danger of trying to recover his position by force. Such is the reasoning *à priori*.

At six o'clock, the large bell tolls the knell of parting day and the call to the Oración, which any who are religious enough can say, wherever they may be, at work or at rest. In the times of more religious strictness, the bell for the Oración, just at dusk, was the signal for prayer in every house and field, and even in the street, and for the benediction from parent to child and master to servant. Now, in the cities, it tolls unnoticed, and on the plantations, it is treated only as the signal for leaving off work. The distribution of provisions is made at the storehouse, by the mayordomo, my host superintending it in person. The people take according to the number in their families; and so well acquainted are all with the apportionment, that in only one or two instances were inquiries necessary. The kitchen fires are lighted in the quarters, and the evening meal is prepared. I went into the quarters before they were closed. A high wall surrounds an open square, in which are the houses of the Negroes. This has one gate, which is locked at dark; and to leave the quarters after that time is a serious offence. The huts were plain, but reasonably neat, and comfortable in their construction and arrangement. In some were fires, round which, even in this hot weather, the Negroes like to gather. A group of little Negroes came round the strange gentleman, and the smallest knelt down with uncovered heads, in a reverent manner, saying, "Buenos días Señor." I did not understand the purpose of this action, and as there was no one to explain the usage to me, I did them the injustice to suppose that they expected money, and distributed some small coins among them. But I learned afterwards that they were expecting the benediction, the hand on the head and the "Dios te haga bueno." It was touching to see their simple, trusting faces turned up to the stranger—countenances not yet wrought by misfortune, or injury, or crime, into the strong expressions of mature life. None of these children, even the smallest, was naked, as one usually sees them in Havana. In one of the huts, a proud mother showed me her Herculean twin boys, sprawling in sleep on the bed. Before dark, the gate of the quarters is bolted, and the night is begun. But the fires of the sugar-house are burning, and half of the working people are on duty there for their six hours.

I sat for several hours with my host and his son, in the veranda, engaged in conversation, agreeable and instructive to me, on those topics likely to present themselves to a person placed as I was—the state of Cuba, its probable future, its past, its relations to Europe and the United States, slavery, the coolie problem, the free-Negro labor problem, and the agriculture, horticulture, trees and fruits of the island. The elder gentleman retired early, as he was to take the early train for Matanzas.

My sleeping-room is large and comfortable, with brick floor and glass windows, pure white bed linen and mosquito net, and ewer and basin scrupulously clean, bringing back, by contrast, visions of Le Grand's, and Antonio, and Domingo, and the sounds and smells of those upper chambers. The only moral I am entitled to draw from this is, that a well-ordered private house with slave labor, may be more neat and creditable than an ill-ordered public house with free labor. As the stillness of the room comes over me, I realize that I am far away in the hill country of Cuba, the guest of a planter, under this strange system, by which one man is enthroned in the labor of another race, brought from across the sea. The song of the Negroes breaks out afresh from the fields, where they are loading up the wagons—that barbaric undulation of sound:

"Na-nú, A-yá,—Na-né, A-yá."

and the recurrence of here and there a few words of Spanish, among which "Mañana" seemed to be a favorite. Once, in the middle of the night, I waked, to hear the strains again, as they worked in the open field, under the stars.

XI

A SUGAR PLANTATION: The Life

When I came out from my chamber this morning, the elder Mr. Chartrand had gone. The watchful negress brought me coffee, and I could choose between oranges and bananas, for my fruit. The young master had been in the saddle an hour or so. I sauntered to the sugar-house. It was past six, and all hands were at work again, amid the perpetual boiling of the caldrons, the skimming and dipping and stirring, the cries of the caldron-men to the firemen, the slow gait of the wagons, and the perpetual to-and-fro of the carriers of the cane. The engine is doing well enough, and the engineer has the great sheet of the New York Weekly Herald, which he is studying, in the intervals of labor, as he sits on the corner of the brickwork.

But a turn in the garden is more agreeable, among birds, and flowers, and aromatic trees. Here is a mignonette tree, forty feet high, and every part is full and fragrant with flowers, as is the little mignonette in our flower-pots. There is the allspice, a large tree, each leaf strong enough to flavor a dish. Here is the tamarind tree: I must sit under it, for the sake of the old song. My young friend joins me, and points out, on the allspice tree, a chameleon. It is about six inches long, and of a pea-green color. He thinks its changes of color, which are no fable, depend on the will or on the sensations, and not on the color of the object the animal rests upon. This one, though on a black trunk, remained pale green. When they take the color of the tree they rest on, it may be to elude their enemies, to whom their slow motions make them an easy prey. At the corner of the house stands a pomegranate tree, full of fruit, which is not yet entirely ripe; but we find enough to give a fair taste of its rich flavor. Then there are sweet oranges, and sour oranges, and limes, and coconuts, and pineapples, the latter not entirely ripe, but in the condition in which they are usually plucked for our market, an abundance of fuchsias, and Cape jasmines, and the highly prized night-blooming cereus.

The most frequent shade-tree here is the mango. It is a large, dense tree, with a general resemblance, in form and size, to our lime or linden. Three noble trees stand before the door, in front of the house. One is a Tahiti almond, another a mango, and the third a cedar. And in the distance is a majestic tree, of incredible size, which is, I believe, a ceiba. When this estate was a cafetal, the house stood at the junction of four avenues, from the four points of the compass: one of the sweet orange, one of the sour orange, one of palms, and one of mangoes. Many of these trees fell in the hurricanes of 1843 and '45. The avenue which leads from the road, and part of that leading towards the sugar-house, are preserved. The rest have fallen a sacrifice to the sugar-cane;

but the garden, the trees about the house, and what remains of the avenues, give still a delightful appearance of shelter and repose.

I have amused myself by tracing the progress, and learning the habits of the red ants, a pretty formidable enemy to all structures of wood. They eat into the heart of the hardest woods; not even the lignum vitæ, or iron-wood, or cedar, being proof against them. Their operations are secret. They never appear upon the wood, or touch its outer shell. A beam or rafter stands as ever with a goodly outside; but you tap it, and find it a shell. Their approaches, too, are by covered ways. When going from one piece of wood to another, they construct a covered way, very small and low, as a protection against their numerous enemies, and through this they advance to their new labors. I think that they may sap the strength of a whole roof of rafters, without the observer being able to see one of them, unless he breaks their covered ways, or lays open the wood.

The course of life at the plantation is after this manner. At six o'clock, the great bell begins the day, and the Negroes go to their work. The house servants bring coffee to the family and guests, as they appear or send for it. The master's horse is at the door, under the tree, as soon as it is light, and he is off on his tour, before the sun rises. The family breakfasts at ten o'clock, and the people—la gente, as the technical phrase is for the laborers, breakfast at nine. The breakfast is like that of the cities, with the exception of fish and the variety of meats, and consists of rice, eggs, fried plantains, mixed dishes of vegetables and fowls, other meats rarely, and fruits, with claret or Catalonia and coffee. The time for the siesta or rest, is between breakfast and dinner. Dinner hour is three for the family, and two for the people. The dinner does not differ much from the breakfast, except that there is less of fruit and more of meat, and that some preserve is usually eaten, as a dessert. Like the breakfast, it ends with coffee. In all manner of preserves, the island is rich. The almond, the guava, the cocoa, the soursop, the orange, the lime, and the mamey apple afford a great variety. After dinner, and before dark, is the time for long drives; and, when the families are on the estates, for visits to neighbors. There is no third meal; but coffee, and sometimes tea, is offered at night. The usual time for bed is as early as ten o'clock, for the day begins early, and the chief out-door works and active recreations must be had before breakfast.

In addition to the family house, the Negro quarters, and the sugar-house, there is a range of stone buildings, ending with a kitchen, occupied by the engineer, the mayoral, the boyero, and the mayordomo, who have an old Negro woman to cook for them, and another to wait on them. There is also another row of stone buildings, comprising the store-house, the penitentiary, the hospital, and the lying-in room. The penitentiary, I have described. The hospital and lying-in room are airy, well-ventilated, and suitable for their purposes. Neither of them had any tenants to-day. In the center of the group of buildings is a high frame, on which hangs the great bell of the plantation. This rings the Negroes up in the morning, and in at night, and sounds the hours for meals. It calls all in, on any special occasion, and is used for an alarm to the neighboring plantations, rung long and loud, in case of fire in the cane-fields, or other occasions for calling in aid.

After dinner, to-day, a volante, with two horses, and a postilion in bright jacket and buckled boots and large silver spurs, the harness well-besprinkled with silver, drove to the door, and an elderly gentleman alighted and came to the house, attired with scrupulous nicety of white cravat and dress coat, and with the manners of the *ancien régime.* This is M. Bourgeoise, the owner of the neighboring large plantation, Santa Catalina, one of the few cafetals remaining in this part of the island. He is too old, and too much attached to his plantation, to change it to a sugar estate; and he is too rich to need the change. He, too, was a refugee from the insurrection of Santo Domingo, but older than M. Chartrand. Not being able to escape, he was compelled to serve as aid-de-camp to Jacques Dessalines. He has a good deal to say about the insurrection and its results, of a great part of which he was an eye-witness. The sight of him brought vividly to mind the high career and sad fate of the just and brave Toussaint L'Ouverture, and the brilliant successes, and fickle, cruel rule, of Dessalines—when French marshals were out-maneuvered by Negro generals, and pitched battles were won by Negroes and mulattoes against European armies.

This gentleman had driven over in the hope of seeing his friend and neighbor, Mr. Chartrand, the elder. He remained with us for some time, sitting under the veranda, the silvered volante and its black horses and black postilion standing under the trees. He invited us to visit his plantation, which I was desirous to do, as a cafetal is a rarity now.

My third day at La Ariadne is much like the preceding days: the early rising, the coffee and fruit, the walk, visits to the mill, the fields, the garden, and the quarters, breakfast, rest in-doors with reading and writing, dinner, out of doors again, and the evening under the veranda, with conversations on subjects now so interesting to me. These conversations, and what I had learned from other persons, open to me new causes for interest and sympathy with my younger host. Born in South Carolina, he secured his rights of birth, and is a citizen of the United States, though all his pecuniary interests and family affections are in Cuba. He went to Paris at the age of nine, and remained there until he was nineteen, devoting the ten years to thorough courses of study in the best schools. He has spent much time in Boston, and has been at sea, to China, India, and the Pacific and California— was wrecked in the Boston ship "Mary Ellen," on a coral reef in the India seas, taken captive, restored, and brought back to Boston in another ship, whence he sailed for California. There he had a long and checkered experience, was wounded in the battle with the Indians who killed Lieut. Dale and defeated his party, was engaged in scientific surveys, topographical and geological, took the fever of the south coast at a remote place, was reported dead, and came to his mother's door, at the spot where we are talking this evening, so weak and sunken that his brothers did not know him, thinking it happiness enough if he could reach his home, to die in his mother's arms. But home and its cherishings, and revived moral force, restored him, and now, active and strong again, when in consequence of the marriage of his brothers and sisters, and the departure of neighbors, the family leave their home of thirty-five years for the city, he becomes the acting master, the administrador of the estate, and makes the old house his bachelor's hall.

An education in Europe or the United States must tend to free the youth of Cuba from the besetting fault of untravelled plantation-masters. They are in no danger of thinking their plantations and Cuba the world, or any great part of it. In such cases, I should think the danger might be rather the other way— rather that of disgust and discouragement at the narrowness of the field, the entire want of a career set before them—a career of any kind, literary, scientific, political, or military. The choice is between expatriation and contentment in the position of a secluded cultivator of sugar by slave labor, with occasional opportunities of intercourse with the world and of foreign travel, with no other field than the limits of the plantation afford, for the exercise of the scientific knowledge, so laboriously acquired, and with no more exciting motive for the continuance of intellectual culture than the general sense of its worth and fitness.

XII

FROM PLANTATION TO PLANTATION

If the master of a plantation is faithful and thorough, will tolerate no misconduct or imposition, and yet is humane and watchful over the interests and rights, as well as over the duties of the Negroes, he has a hard and anxious life. Sickness to be ministered to, the feigning of sickness to be counteracted, rights of the slaves to be secured against other Negroes, as well as against whites, with a poor chance of getting at the truth from either; the obligations of the Negro *quasi* marriage to be enforced against all the sensual and childish tendencies of the race; theft and violence and wanderings from home to be detected and prevented; the work to be done, and yet no one to be over-worked; and all this often with no effectual aid, often with only obstructions, from the intermediate whites! Nor is it his own people only that are to be looked to. The thieving and violence of Negroes from other plantations, their visits by night against law, and the encroachments of the neighboring free blacks and low whites, are all to be watched and prevented or punished. The master is a policeman, as well as an economist and a judge. His revolver and rifle are always loaded. He has his dogs, his trackers and seizers, that lie at his gate, trained to give the alarm when a strange step comes near the house or the quarters, and ready to pursue. His hedges may be broken down, his cane trampled or cut, or, still worse, set fire to, goats let into his pastures, his poultry stolen, and sometimes his dogs poisoned. It is a country of little law and order, and what with slavery and free Negroes and low whites, violence or fraud are imminent and always formidable. No man rides far unarmed. The Negroes are held under the subjection of force. A quarter-deck organization is established. The master owns vessel and cargo, and is captain of the ship, and he and his family live in the cabin and hold the quarter-deck. There are no other commissioned officers on board, and no guard of marines. There are a few petty officers, and under all, a great crew of Negroes, for every kind of work, held by compulsion—the results of a press-gang. All are at sea together. There are some laws, and civil authorities for the protection of each, but not very near, nor always accessible.

After dinner to-day, we take saddle-horses for a ride to Santa Catalina. Necessary duties in the field and mill delay us, and we are in danger of not being able to visit the house, as my friend must be back in season for the close of work and the distribution of provisions, in the absence of his mayoral. The horses have the famous "march," as it is called, of the island, an easy rapid step, something like pacing, and delightful for a quiet ride under a soft afternoon sky, among flowers and sweet odors. I have seen but few trotting horses in Cuba.

The afternoon is serene. Near, the birds are flying, or chattering with extreme sociability in close trees, and the thickets are fragrant with flowers; while far off, the high hills loom in the horizon; and all about us is this tropical growth, with which I cannot yet become familiar, of palms and cocoas and bananas. We amble over the red earth of the winding lanes, and turn into the broad avenue of Santa Catalina, with its double row of royal palms. We are in—not a forest, for the trees are not thick and wild and large enough for that—but in a huge, dense, tropical orchard. The avenue is as clear and straight and wide as a city mall; while all the ground on either side, for hundreds of acres, is a plantation of oranges and limes, bananas and plantains, cocoas and pineapples, and of cedar and mango, mignonette and allspice, under whose shade is growing the green-leaved, the evergreen-leaved coffee plant, with its little dark red berry, the tonic of half the world. Here we have a glimpse of the lost charm of Cuba. No wonder that the aged proprietor cannot find the heart to lay it waste for the monotonous cane-field, and make the quiet, peaceful horticulture, the natural growth of fruit and berry, and the simple processes of gathering, drying, and storing, give place to the steam and smoke and drive and life-consuming toil of the ingenio!

At a turn in the avenue, we come upon the proprietor, who is taking his evening walk, still in the exact dress and with the exact manners of urban life. With truly French politeness, he is distressed, and all but offended, that we cannot go to his house. It is my duty to insist on declining his invitation, for I know that Chartrand is anxious to return. At another turn, we come upon a group of little black children, under the charge of a decent, matronly mulatto, coming up a shaded footpath, which leads among the coffee. Chartrand stops to give a kind word to them.

But it is sunset, and we must turn about. We ride rather rapidly down the avenue, and along the highway, where we meet several travellers, nearly all with pistols in their holsters, and one of the mounted police, with carbine and sword; and then cross the brook, pass through the little, mean hamlet of Limonar, whose inmates are about half blacks and half whites, but once a famed resort for invalids, and enter our own avenue, and thence to the house. On our way, we pass a burying-ground, which my companion says he is ashamed to have me see. Its condition is bad enough. The planters are taxed for it, but the charge of it is with the padre, who takes big fees for burials, and lets it go to ruin. The bell has rung long ago, but the people are waiting our return, and the evening duties of distributing food, turning on the night gang for night work, and closing the gates are performed.

To-night the hounds have an alarm, and Chartrand is off in the darkness. In a few minutes he returns. There has been some one about, but nothing is discovered. A Negro may have attempted to steal out, or some strange Negro may be trying to steal in, or some prowling white, or free black, has been reconnoitering. These are the terms on which this system is carried on; and I think, too, that when the tramp of horses is heard after dark, and strange men ride towards the piazza, it causes some uneasiness.

The morning of the fourth day, I take my leave, by early train for Matanzas. The hour is half-past six; but the habits of rising are so early that it requires no special preparation. I have time for coffee, for a last visit to the sugar-house, a good-by to the engineer, who will be back on the banks of the Merrimack in May, and for a last look into the quarters, to gather the little group of kneelers for "la benedición," with their "Buenos días, Señor." My horse is ready, the Negro has gone with my luggage, and I must take my leave of my newly-made friend. Alone together, we have been more intimate in three days than we should have been in as many weeks in a full household. Adios!—May the opening of a new home on the old spot, which I hear is awaiting you, be the harbinger of a more cheerful life, and the creation of such fresh ties and interests, that the delightful air of the hill country of Cuba, the dreamy monotony of the day, the serenity of nights which seem to bring the stars down to your roof or to raise you half-way to them, and the luxuriance and variety of vegetable and animal life, may not be the only satisfactions of existence here.

A quiet amble over the red earth, to the station, in a thick morning mist, almost cold enough to make an overcoat comfortable; and, after two hours on the rail, I am again in Matanzas, among close-packed houses, and with views of blue ocean and of ships.

XIII

MATANZAS AND ENVIRONS

Instead of the posada by the water-side, I take up my quarters at a hotel kept by Ensor, an American, and his sister. Here the hours, cooking, and chief arrangements are in the fashion of the country, as they should be, but there is more of that attention to guests which we are accustomed to at home than the Cuban hotels usually give.

The objects to be visited here are the Cumbre and the valley of the Yumurí. It is too late for a morning ride, and I put off my visit until afternoon. Gazzaniga and some of the opera troupe are here; and several Americans at the hotel, who were at the opera last night, tell me that the people of Matanzas made a handsome show, and are of opinion that there was more beauty in the boxes than we saw at the Villanueva. It appears, too, that at the Retreta, in the Plaza de Armas, when the band plays, and at evening promenades, the ladies walk about, and do not keep to their carriages as in Havana.

As soon as the sun began to decline, I set off for the Cumbre, mounted on a pacer, with a Negro for a guide, who rode, as I soon discovered, a better nag than mine. We cross the stone bridges, and pass the great hospital, which dominates over the town. A regiment, dressed in seersucker and straw hats, is drilling, by trumpet call, and drilling well, too, on the green in front of the barracks while we take our winding way up the ascent of the Cumbre.

The bay, town, and shipping lie beneath us; the Pan rises in the distance to the height of some 3,000 feet; the ocean is before us, rolling against the outside base of the hills; and, on the inside, lies the deep, rich, peaceful valley of the Yumurí. On the top of the Cumbre, commanding the noblest view of ocean and valley, bay and town, is the ingenio of a Mr. Jenkes, a merchant bearing a name that would put Spanish tongues to their trumps to sound, were it not that they probably take refuge in the Don Guillermo, or Don Enrique, of his Christian name. The estate bears the name of La Victoria, and is kindly thrown open to visitors from the city. It is said to be a model establishment. The house is large, in a classic style, and costly, and the Negro quarters, the store-houses, mechanic shops, and sugar-house are of dimensions indicating an estate of the first class.

On the way up from the city, several fine points of sight were occupied by villas, all of one story, usually in the Roman or Grecian style, surrounded by gardens and shade-trees, and with every appearance of taste and wealth.

It is late, but I must not miss the Yumurí; so we dive down the short, steep descent, and cross dry brooks and wet brooks, and over stones, and along bridle-paths, and over fields without paths, and by wretched hovels, and a few decent cottages, with yelping dogs and cackling hens and staring children, and between high, overhanging cliffs, and along the side of a still lake, and after it is so dark that we can hardly see stones or paths, we strike a bridle-path, and then come out upon the road, and, in a few minutes more, are among the gas-lights and noises of the city.

At the hotel, there is a New York company who have spent the day at the Yumurí, and describe a cave not yet fully explored, which is visited by all who have time—abounding in stalactites, and, though much smaller, reminding one of the Mammoth Cave of Kentucky.

I cannot leave Matanzas without paying my respects to the family to whose kindness I owe so much. Mr. Chartrand lives in a part of the suburbs called Versailles, near the barracks, in a large and handsome house, built after the style of the country. There I spend an agreeable evening, at a gathering of nearly all the family, sons and daughters, and the sons-in-law and daughters-in-law. There is something strangely cosmopolitan in many of the Cuban families—as in this, where are found French origin, Spanish and American intermarriage, education in Europe or the United States, home and property in Cuba, friendships and sympathies and half a residence in Boston or New York or Charleston, and three languages at command.

Here I learn that the Thirty Millions Bill has not passed, and, by the latest dates, is not likely to pass.

My room at Ensor's is on a level with the court-yard, and a horse puts its face into the grating as I am dressing, and I know of nothing to prevent his walking in at the door, if he chooses, so that the Negro may finish rubbing him down by my looking-glass. Yet the house is neatly furnished and cared for, and its keepers are attentive and deserving people.

XIV

REFLECTIONS VIA RAILROAD

Although the distance to Havana, as the bird flies, is only sixty miles, the railroad, winding into the interior, to draw out the sugar freights, makes a line of nearly one hundred miles. This adds to the length of our journey, but also greatly to its interest.

In the cars are two Americans, who have also been visiting plantations. They give me the following statistics of a sugar plantation, which they think may be relied upon. Lands, machinery, 320 slaves, and 20 coolies, worth $500,000. Produce this year, 4,000 boxes of sugar and 800 casks of molasses, worth $104,000. Expenses, $35,000. Net, $69,000, or about 14 per cent. This is not a large interest on an investment so much of which is perishable and subject to deterioration.

The day, as has been every day of mine in Cuba, is fair and beautiful. The heat is great, perhaps even dangerous to a Northerner, should he be exposed to it in active exercise, at noon—but, with the shade and motion of the cars, not disagreeable, for the air is pure and elastic, and it is only the direct heat of the sun that is oppressive. I think one notices the results of this pure air, in the throats and nasal organs of the people. One seldom meets a person that seems to have a cold in the head or the throat; and pocket handkerchiefs are used chiefly for ornament.

I cannot weary of gazing upon these new and strange scenes; the stations, with the groups of peasants and Negroes and fruit-sellers that gather about them, and the stores of sugar and molasses collected there; the ingenios, glimmering in the heat of the sun, with their tall furnace chimneys; the cane-fields, acres upon acres; the slow ox-carts carrying the cane to the mill; then the intervals of unused country, the jungles, adorned with little wild flowers, the groves of the weeping, drooping, sad, homesick cocoa; the royal palm, which is to trees what the camel or dromedary is among animals seeming to have strayed from Nubia or Mesopotamia; the stiff, close orange tree, with its golden balls of fruit; and then the remains of a cafetal, the coffee plant growing untrimmed and wild under the reprieved groves of plantain and banana.

It is certainly true that there is such a thing as industry in the tropics. The labor of the tropics goes on. Notwithstanding all we hear and know of the enervating influence of the climate, the white man, if not laborious himself, is the cause that labor is in others. With all its social and political discouragements, with the disadvantages of a duty of about twenty-five per cent on its sugars laid in the United States, and a duty of full one hundred per cent on all flour imported from the United States, and after paying heavier taxes than any people on earth pay at this moment, and yielding a revenue, which nets, after every deduction and discount, not less than sixteen millions a year—against all these disadvantages, this island is still very productive and very rich. There is, to be sure, little variety in its industry. In the country, it is nothing but the raising and making of sugar; and in the towns, it is the selling and exporting of sugar. With the addition of a little coffee and copper, more tobacco, and some fresh fruit and preserves, and the commerce which they stimulate, and the mechanic and trading necessities of the towns, we have the sum of its industry and resources. Science, arts, letters, arms, manufactures, and the learning and discussions of politics, of theology, and of the great problems and opinions that move the minds of the thinking world—in these, the people of Cuba have no part. These move by them, as the great Gulf Stream drifts by their shores. Nor is there, nor has there been in Cuba, in the memory of the young and middle-aged, debate, or vote, or juries, or one of the least and most rudimental processes of self-government. The African and Chinese do the manual labor, the Cubans hold the land and the capital, and direct the agricultural industry; the commerce is shared between the Cubans, and foreigners of all nations; and the government, civil and military, is exercised by the citizens of Old Spain. No Cuban votes, or attends a lawful political meeting, or sits on a jury, or sees a law-making assembly, except as a curiosity abroad, even in a municipality; nor has he ever helped to make, or interpret, or administer laws, or borne arms, except by special license of government granted to such as are friends of government. In religion, he has no choice, except between the Roman Catholic and none. The laws that govern him are made abroad, and administered by a central power, a foreign Captain-General, through the agency of foreign civil and military officers. The Cuban has no public career. If he removes to Old Spain, and is known as a supporter of Spanish royal power, his Creole birth is probably no impediment to him. But at home, as a Cuban, he may be a planter, a merchant, a physician, but he cannot expect to be a civil magistrate, or to hold a commission in the army, or an office in the police; and though he may be a lawyer, and read, sitting, a written argument to a court of judges, he cannot expect to be himself a judge. He may publish a book, but the government must be the responsible author. He may edit a journal, but the government must be the editor-in-chief.

At the chief stations on the road, there are fruit-sellers in abundance, with fruit fresh from the trees: oranges, bananas, sapotes, and coconuts. The coconut is eaten at an earlier stage than that in which we see it at the North, for it is gathered for exportation after it has become hard. It is eaten here when no harder than a melon, and is cut through with a knife, and the soft white pulp, mixed with the milk, is eaten with a spoon. It is luscious and wholesome, much more so than when the rind has hardened into the shell, and the soft pulp into a hard meat.

A little later in the afternoon, the character of the views begins to change. The ingenios and cane-fields become less frequent, then cease altogether, and the houses have more the appearance of pleasure retreats than of working estates. The roads show lines of mules and horses, loaded with panniers of fruits, or sweeping the ground with the long stalks of fresh fodder laid across their backs, all moving towards a common center. Pleasure carriages appear. Next comes the distant view of the Castle of Atares, and the Príncipe, and then the harbor and the sea, the belt of masts, the high ridge of fortifications, the blue and white and yellow houses, with brown tops; and now we are in the streets of Havana.

Here are the familiar signs—Por mayor y menor, Posada y Cantina, Tienda, Panadería, Relojería, and the fanciful names of the shops, the high-pitched falsetto cries of the streets, the long files of mules and horses, with panniers of fruit, or hidden, all but their noses and tails, under stacks of fresh fodder, the volantes, and the motley multitude of whites, blacks, and Chinese, soldiers and civilians, and occasionally priests—Negro women, lottery-ticket vendors, and the girl musicians with their begging tambourines.

The same idlers are at the door of Le Grand's; a rehearsal, as usual, is going on at the head of the first flight; and the parrot is blinking at the hot, white walls of the court-yard, and screaming bits of Spanish. My New York friends have got back from the country a day before me. I am installed in a better room than before, on the house-top, where the sun is hot, but where there is air and a view of the ocean.

XV

HAVANA: Social, Religious and Judicial Tidbits

The warm bath round the corner is a refreshment after a day's railroad ride in such heat; and there, in the front room, the man in his shirt sleeves is serving out liquor, as before, and the usual company of Creoles is gathered about the billiard tables. After a dinner in the handsome, airy restaurant of Le Grand's, I drive into the city in the evening, to the close streets of the Extramuros, and pay a visit to the lady whom I failed to see on my arrival. I am so fortunate as to meet her, and beside the pleasure to be found in her society, I am glad to be able to give her personal information from her attached and sympathizing friends, at the North.

While I am there, a tinkling sound of bells is heard in the streets, and lights flash by. It is a procession, going to carry the viaticum, the last sacrament, to a dying person.

From this house, I drove towards the water-side, past the Plaza de Armas, the old Plaza de San Francisco, with its monastery turned into an almacén (a store-house of merchandise,) through the Calle de los Oficios, to the boarding-house of Madame Almy, to call upon Dr. and Mrs. Howe. Mr. Parker left Havana, as he intended, last Tuesday, for Santa Cruz. He found Havana rather too hot for his comfort, and Santa Cruz, the most healthful and temperate of the islands, had always been his destination. He had visited a few places in the city, and among others, the College of Belén, where he had been courteously received by the Jesuits. I found that they knew his reputation as a scholar and writer, and a leading champion of modern Theism in America. Dr. Howe had called at Le Grand's, yesterday, to invite me to go with him to attend a trial, at the Audiencia, which attracted a good deal of interest among the Creoles. The story, as told by the friends of Señor Maestri, the defendant, is that in the performance of a judicial duty, he discharged a person against whom the government was proceeding illegally, and that this lead to a correspondence between him and the authorities, which resulted in his being deposed and brought to trial, before the Audiencia, on a charge of disrespect to the Captain-General. I have no means of learning the correctness of this statement, at present—

"I say the tale as 'twas said to me."

The cause has, at all events, excited a deep interest among the Creoles, who see in it another proof of the unlimited character of the centralized power that governs them. I regret that I missed a scene of so much interest and instruction. Dr. Howe told me that Maestri's counsel, Señor Azcárate, a young lawyer, defended his friend courageously; but the evidence being all in writing, without the exciting conflicts and vicissitudes of oral testimony, and the written arguments being delivered sitting; there was not much in the proceedings to stimulate the Creole excitability. No decision was given, the Court taking time to deliberate. It seems to have been a Montalembert trial, on a small theater.

To-night there is again a máscara at the next door, but my room is now more remote, and I am able to sleep through it. Once I awoke. It was nearly five o'clock. The music was still going on, but in softer and more subdued tones. The drums and trumpets were hushed, and all had fallen, as if by the magic touch of the approaching dawn, into a trance of sound, a rondo of constantly returning delicious melody, as nearly irresistible to the charmed sense as sound can be conceived to be—just bordering on the fusing state between sense and spirit. It is a contradanza of Cuba. The great bells beat five, over the city; and instantly the music ceases, and is heard no more. The watchmen cry the hour, and the bells of the hospitals and convents sound their matins, though it is yet dark.

XVI

HAVANA: Worship, Etiquette and Humanitarianism

At break of day, I am in the delightful sea-baths again, not ill-named Recreo and Elíseo. But the forlorn chain-gang are mustered before the Presidio. It is Sunday, but there is no day of rest for them.

At eight o'clock I present myself at the Belén. A lady, who was passing through the cloister, with head and face covered by the usual black veil, turned and came to me. It was Mrs.——, whom I had seen last evening. She kindly took me to the sacristy, and asked some one to tell Father—— that I was there, and then went to her place in church. While waiting in the sacristy, I saw the robing and unrobing of the officiating priests, the preparation of altar ceremonials by boys and men, and could hear the voices and music in the church, on the other side of the great altar. The manner of the Jesuits is in striking contrast with that at the Cathedral. All is slow, orderly and reverential, whether on the part of men or boys. Instead of the hurried walk, the nod and duck, there is a slow march, a kneeling, or a reverential bow. At a small side altar, in the sacristy, communion is administered by a single priest. Among the recipients are several men of mature years and respectable position; and side by side with them, the poor and the Negroes. In the Church, there is no distinction of race or color.

Father—— appears, is unrobed, and takes me to the gallery of the church, near the organ. From this, I looked down upon a sea of rich costumes of women, veiled heads, and kneeling figures, literally covering the floor of the church. On the marble pavement, the little carpets are spread, and on these, as close as they can sit or kneel, are the ladies of rank and wealth of Havana. A new-comer glides in among them seeking room for her carpet, or room of charity or friendship on a carpet already spread; and the kneelers or sitters move and gather in their wide skirts to let her pass. Here and there a servant in livery winds his way behind his mistress, bearing her carpet, and returns to the porch when it has been spread. The whole floor is left to women. The men gather about the walls and doorways, or sit in the gallery, which is reserved for them. But among the women, though chiefly of rank and wealth, are some who are Negroes, usually distinguished by the plain shawl, instead of the veil over the head. The Countess Villanueva, immensely rich, of high rank, and of a name great in the annals of Cuba, but childless, and blind, and a widow, is lead in by the hand by her Negro servant. The service of the altar is performed with dignity and reverence, and the singing, which is by the Jesuit Brothers themselves, is admirable. In the choir I recognized my new friends, the Rector and young Father Cabre, the professor of physics. The

"Tantum ergo Sacramentum," which was sung kneeling, brought tears into my eyes, and kept them there.

After service, Mr.—— came to me, and made an engagement to show me the benevolent institutions on the Bishop's list, accepting my invitation to breakfast at Le Grand's, at eleven o'clock. At eleven he came, and after a quiet breakfast in a side room, we went to the house of Señor——, whom he well knows, in the hope that he would go with us. The Señor was engaged to meet one of the Fathers at noon, and could not go, but introduced to me a relative of his, a young student of medicine in the University, who offered to take me to the Presidio and other places, the next day.

It occurred to us to call upon a young American lady, who was residing at the house of a Spanish lady of wealth and rank, and invite her to go with us to see the Beneficencia, which we thought she might do, as it is an institution under the charge of nuns, and she was to go with a Padre in full dress. But the customs of the country are rigid. Miss—— was very desirous to go, but had doubts. She consulted the lady of the house, who would know, if any one could, the etiquette of Havana. The Señora's reply was, "You are an American, and may do anything." This settled the matter in the negative, and we went alone. Now we drive to Don Juan—— 's. The gate is closed. The driver, who is a white, gets off and makes a feeble and timid rap at the door. "Knock louder!" says my friend, in Spanish. "What cowards they are!" he adds to me. The man makes a knock, a little louder. "There, see that! Peeking into the keyhole! Mean! An Englishman would beat the door down before he would do that." Don Juan is in the country, so we fail of all our expected companions.

The Casa de Beneficencia is a large institution, for orphan and destitute children, for infirm old persons, and for the insane. It is admirably situated, bordering on the open sea, with fresh air and very good attention to ventilation in the rooms. It is a government institution, but is placed under charge of the Sisters of Charity, one of whom accompanied us about the building. Though called a government institution, it must not be supposed that it is a charity from the crown. On the contrary, it is supported by a specific appropriation of certain of the taxes and revenues of the island. In the building is a church not yet finished, large enough for all the inmates, and a quiet little private chapel for the Sisters' devotions, where a burning lamp indicated the presence of the Sacrament on the small altar. I am sorry to have forgotten the number of children. It was large, and included both sexes, with a separate department for each. In a third department are the insane. They are kindly treated and not confined, except when violent; but the Sister told us they had no medical treatment unless in case of sickness. (Dr. Howe told me that he was also so informed.) The last department is for aged and indigent women.

One of the little orphans clung to the Sister who accompanied us, holding her hand, and nestling in her coarse but clean blue gown; and when we took our leave, and I put a small coin into her little soft hand, her eyes brightened up into a pretty smile.

The number of the Sisters is not full. As none have joined the order from Cuba, (I am told literally none,) they are all from abroad, chiefly from France and Spain; and having acclimation to go through, with exposure to yellow fever and cholera, many of those that come here die in the first or second summer. And yet they still come, in simple, religious fidelity, under the shadow of death.

The Casa de Beneficencia must be pronounced by all, even by those accustomed to the system and order of the best charitable institutions in the world, a credit to the island of Cuba. The charity is large and liberal, and the order and neatness of its administration are beyond praise.

From the Beneficencia we drove to the Military Hospital. This is a huge establishment, designed to accommodate all the sick of the army. The walls are high, the floors are of brick and scrupulously clean, as are all things under the charge of the Sisters of Charity; and the ventilation is tolerable. The building suffered from the explosion of the magazine last year, and some quarters have not yet been restored for occupation. The number of sick soldiers now in hospital actually exceeds one thousand! Most of them are young, some mere lads, victims of the conscription of Old Spain, which takes them from their rustic homes in Andalusia and Catalonia and the Pyrenees, to expose them to the tropical heats of Cuba, and to the other dangers of its climate. Most had fevers. We saw a few cases of vómito. Notwithstanding all that is said about the healthfulness of a winter in Cuba, the experienced Sister Servant (which, I believe, is the title of the Superior of a body of Sisters of Charity) told us that a few sporadic cases of yellow fever occur in Havana, in all seasons of the year; but that we need not fear to go through the wards. One patient was covered with the blotches of recent smallpox. It was affecting to see the wistful eyes of these poor, fevered soldier-boys, gazing on the serene, kind countenances of the nuns, and thinking of their mothers and sisters in the dear home in Old Spain, and feeling, no doubt, that this womanly, religious care was the nearest and best substitute.

The present number of Sisters, charged with the entire care of this great hospital, except the duty of cooks and the mere manual and mechanic labor necessarily done by men, is not above twenty-five. The Sister Servant told us that the proper complement was forty. The last summer, eleven of these devoted women died of yellow fever. Every summer, when yellow fever or cholera prevails, some of them die. They know it. Yet the vacancies are filled up; and their serene and ever happy countenances give the stranger no indication that they have bound themselves to the bedside of contagious and loathsome diseases every year, and to scenes of sickness and death every day.

As we walked through the passage-ways, we came upon the little private chapel of the Sisters. Here was a scene I can never forget. It was an hour assigned for prayer. All who could leave the sick wards—not more than twelve or fourteen—were kneeling in that perfectly still, secluded, darkened room, in a double row, all facing to the altar, on which burned one taper, showing the presence of the Sacrament, and all in silent prayer. That double row of silent, kneeling women, unconscious of the presence of any one, in their snow-white, close caps and long capes, and coarse, clean, blue gowns— heroines, if the world ever had heroines, their angels beholding the face of their Father in heaven, as they knelt on earth!

It was affecting and yet almost amusing—it would have been amusing anywhere else—that these simple creatures, not knowing the ways of the world, and desirous to have soft music fill their room, as they knelt at silent prayer, and not having (for their duties preclude it) any skill in the practice of music, had a large music-box wound and placed on a stand, in the rear, giving out its liquid tones, just loud enough to pervade the air, without forcing attention. The effect was beautiful; and yet the tunes were not all, nor chiefly, religious. They were such as any music-box would give. But what do these poor creatures know of what the world marches to, or dances to, or makes love by? To them it was all music, and pure and holy!

Minute after minute we stood, waiting for, but not desiring, an end of these delightful sounds, and a dissolving of this spell of silent adoration. One of the Sisters began prayers aloud, a series of short prayers and adorations and thanksgivings, to each of which, at its close, the others made response in full, sweet voices. The tone of prayer of this Sister was just what it should be. No skill of art could reach it. How much truer than the cathedral, or the great ceremonial! It was low, yet audible, composed, reverent: neither the familiar, which offends so often, nor the rhetorical, which always offends, but that unconscious sustained intonation, not of speech, but of music, which frequent devotions in company with others naturally call out; showing us that poetry and music, and not prose and speech, are the natural expressions of the deepest and highest emotions.

They rose, with the prayer of benediction, and we withdrew. They separated, to station themselves, one in each ward of the hospital, there, aloud and standing, to repeat their prayers—the sick men raising themselves on their elbows, or sitting in bed, or, if more feeble, raising their eyes and clasping their hands, and all who can or choose, joining in the responses.

XVII

HAVANA: Hospital and Prison

Drove out over the Paseo de Tacón to the Cerro, a height, formerly a village, now a part of the suburbs of Havana. It is high ground, and commands a noble view of Havana and the sea. Coming in, I met the Bishop, who introduced me to the Count de la Fernandina, a dignified Spanish nobleman, who owns a beautiful villa on this Paseo, where we walked a while in the grounds. This house is very elegant and costly, with marble floors, high ceilings, piazzas, and a garden of the richest trees and flowers coming into the court-yard, and advancing even into the windows of the house. It is one of the most beautiful villas in the vicinity of Havana.

There are several noblemen who have their estates and titles in Cuba, but are recognized as nobles of Spain—in all, I should say, about fifty or sixty. Some of these have received their titles for civil or military services; but most of them have been raised to their rank on account of their wealth, or have purchased their titles outright. I believe there are but two grades, the marquis and the count. Among the titles best known to strangers are Villanueva, Fernandina, and O'Reilly. The number of Irish families who have taken rank in the Spanish service and become connected with Cuba, is rather remarkable. Beside O'Reilly, there are O'Donnel, O'Farrel, and O'Lawlor, descendants of Irishmen who entered the Spanish service after the battle of the Boyne.

Dr. Howe had seen the Presidio, the great prison of Havana, once; but was desirous to visit it again; so he joined me, under the conduct of our young friend, Señor——, to visit that and the hospital of San Juan de Dios. The hospital we saw first. It is supported by the government—that is to say, by Cuban revenues—for charity patients chiefly, but some, who can afford it, pay more or less. There are about two hundred and fifty patients. This, again, is in the charge of the Sisters of Charity. As we came upon one of the Sisters, in a passage-way, in her white cap and cape, and black and blue dress, Dr. Howe said, "I always take off my hat to a Sister of Charity," and we paid them all that attention, whenever we passed them. Dr. Howe examined the book of prescriptions, and said that there was less drugging than he supposed there would be. The attending physician told us that nearly all the physicians had studied in Paris, or in Philadelphia. There were a great many medical students in attendance, and there had just been an operation in the theater. In an open yard we saw two men washing a dead body, and carelessly laying it on a table, for dissection. I am told that the medical and surgical professions are in a very satisfactory state of advancement in the island, and that a degree in medicine, and a license to practise, carry with them proofs of considerable proficiency. It is always observable that the physical and the exact sciences are the last to suffer under despotisms.

The Presidio and Grand Cárcel of Havana is a large building, of yellow stone, standing near the fort of the Punta, and is one of the striking objects as you enter the harbor. It has no appearance of a jail without, but rather of a palace or court; but within, it is full of live men's bones and of all uncleanness. No man, whose notions are derived from an American or English penitentiary of the last twenty years, or fifty years, can form an idea of the great Cuban prison. It is simply horrible. There are no cells, except for solitary confinement of "incomunicados"—who are usually political offenders. The prisoners are placed in large rooms, with stone floors and grated windows, where they are left, from twenty to fifty in each, without work, without books, without interference or intervention of any one, day and night, day and night, for the weeks, months or years of their sentences. The sights are dreadful. In this hot climate, so many beings, with no provision for ventilation but the grated windows—so unclean, and most of them naked above the waist—all spend their time in walking, talking, playing, and smoking; and, at night, without bed or blanket, they lie down on the stone floor, on what clothes they may have, to sleep if they can. The whole prison, with the exception of the few cells for the "incomunicados," was a series of these great cages, in which human beings were shut up. Incarceration is the beginning, middle and end of the whole system. Reformation, improvement, benefit to soul or body, are not thought of. We inquired carefully, both of the officer who was sent to attend us, and of a capitán de partido, who was there, and were positively assured that the only distinction among the prisoners was determined by the money they paid. Those who can pay nothing, are left to the worst. Those who can pay two reals (twenty-five cents) a day, are placed in wards a little higher and better. Those who can pay six reals (seventy-five cents) a day, have better places still, called the "Salas de distinción," and some privileges of walking in the galleries. The amount of money, and not the degree of criminality, determines the character of the punishment. There seems to be no limit to the right of the prisoners to talk with any whom they can get to hear them, at whatever distance, and to converse with visitors, and to receive money from them. In fact, the whole scene was a Babel. All that was insured was that they should not escape. When I say that no work was done, I should make the qualification that a few prisoners were employed in rolling tobacco into cigars, for a contractor; but they were very few. Among the prisoners was a capitán de partido (a local magistrate), who was committed on a charge of conniving at the slave-trade. He could pay his six reals, of course; and had the privileges of a "Sala de distinción" and of the galleries. He walked about with us, cigar in mouth, and talked freely, and gave us much information respecting the prison. My last request was to see the garrotte; but it was refused me.

It was beginning to grow dark before we got to the gate, which was duly opened to us, and we passed out, with a good will, into the open air. Dr. Howe said he was nowise reluctant to be outside. It seemed to bring back to his mind his Prussian prison, a little too forcibly to be agreeable. He felt as if he were in keeping again, and was thinking how he should feel if, just as we got to the gate, an officer were to bow and say, "Dr. Howe?" "Yes, sir." "You may remain here. There is a charge against you of seditious language, since you have been in the island." No man would meet such a danger more calmly, and say less about it, than he, if he thought duty to his fellow-beings called him to it.

The open air, the chainless ocean, and the ships freely coming and going, were a pleasant change to the eye, even of one who had never suffered bonds for conscience sake. It seemed strange to see that all persons outside were doing as they pleased.

XVIII

HAVANA: Bullfight

A bullfight has been advertised all over the town, at the Plaza de Toros. Shall we go? I would not, if it were only pleasure that I was seeking. As I am sure I expect only the contrary, and wish merely to learn the character of this national recreation, I will go.

The Plaza de Toros is a wooden amphitheater, in the suburbs, open at the top—a circle of rising seats, with the arena in the center. I am late. The cries of the people inside are loud, sharp, and constant; a full band is blowing its trumpets and beating its drums; and the late stragglers are jostling for their tickets. I go through at a low door, find myself under benches filled with an eager, stamping, shouting multitude, make my way through a passage, and come out on the shady side, for it is a late afternoon sun, and take my place at a good point of view. A bull, with some blood about his fore-quarters and two or three darts (banderillas) sticking in his neck, is trotting harmlessly about the arena, "more sinned against than sinning," and seeming to have no other desire than to get out. Two men, each carrying a long, stout, wooden pole, pointed with a short piece of iron, not long enough to kill, but only to drive off and to goad, are mounted on two of the sorriest nags eyes ever beheld—reprieved jades, whom it would not pay to feed and scarcely pay to kill, and who have been left to take their chances of death here. They could hardly be pricked into a trot, and were too weak to escape. I have seen horses in every stage of life and in every degree of neglect, but no New York Negro hack-driver would have taken these for a gift, if he were obliged to keep them. The bull could not be said to run away from the horses, for they did not pursue; but when, distracted by sights and sounds, he came against a horse, the horse stood still to be gored, and the bull only pushed against him with his head, until driven off by the punching of the iron-pointed pole of the horseman.

Around the arena are sentry-boxes, each large enough to hold two men, behind which they can easily jump, but which the bull cannot enter; and from these, the cowardly wretches run out, flourish a red cloth at the bull, and jump back. Three or four men, with darts in hand, run before the bull, entice him by flapping their red cloths, and, as he trots up to them, stick banderillas into his neck. These torment the bull, and he tries to shake them off, and paws the ground; but still he shows no fight. He trots to the gate, and snuffs to get out. Some of the multitude cry "Fuera el toro! Fuera el toro!" which means that he is a failure, and must be let out at the gate. Others are excited, and cry for the killer, the matador; and a demoniacal scene follows, of yells and shouts, half drowned by twenty or thirty drums and trumpets. The cries to go on prevail; and the matador appears, dressed in a tight-fitting suit of green small-clothes, with a broad silver stripe, jerkin, and stockings—a tall, light-complexioned, elegantly made, glittering man, bearing in one hand a long, heavy, dull black sword, and in the other a broad, red cloth. Now comes the harrying and distracting of the bull by flags, and red cloths, and darts; the matador runs before, flings his cloth up and down; the bull trots towards it— no furious rush, or maddened dash, but a moderate trot—the cloth is flashed over his face and one skilfully directed lunge of the sword into his back neck, and he drops instantly dead at the feet of the matador, at the very spot where he received the stab. Frantic shouts of applause follow; and the matador bows around, like an applauded circus-rider, and retires. The great gate opens, and three horses abreast are driven in, decked with ribbons, to drag the bull round the arena. But they are such feeble animals that, with all the flourish of music and the whipping of drivers, they are barely able to tug the bull along over the tan, in a straight line for the gate, through which the sorry pageant and harmless bull disappear.

Now, some meager, hungry, sallow, sweaty, mean-looking degenerates of Spain jump in and rake over the arena, and cover up the blood, and put things to rights again; and I find time to take a view of the company. Thankful I am, and creditable it is, that there are no women. Yes, there are two mulatto women in a seat on the sunny side, which is the cheap side. And there are two shrivelled, dark, Creole women, in a box; and there is one girl of eight or ten years, in full dress, with an elderly man. These are all the women. In the State Box, under the faded royal arms, are a few officials, not of high degree. The rest of the large company is a motley collection, chiefly of the middle or lower classes, mostly standing on the benches, and nearly all smoking.

The music beats and brays again, the great gates open, and another bull rushes in, distracted by sights and sounds so novel, and for a few minutes shows signs of power and vigor; but, as he becomes accustomed to the scene, he tames down; and after several minutes of flaunting of cloths and flags, and piercing with darts, and punching with the poles of the horsemen, he runs under the poor white horse, and upsets him, but leaves him unhurt by his horns; has a leisurely trial of endurance with the red horse, goring him a little with one horn, and receiving the pike of the driver—the horse helpless and patient, and the bull very reasonable and temperate in the use of his power—and then is enticed off by flags, and worried with darts; and, at last, a new matador appears—a fierce-looking fellow, dressed in dark green, with a large head of curling, snaky, black hair, and a skin almost black. He makes a great strut and flourish, and after two or three unsuccessful attempts to get the bull head on, at length, getting a fair chance, plunges his black sword to the hilt in the bull's neck—but there is no fall of the bull. He has missed the spinal cord and the bull trots off, bleeding in a small stream, with a sword-handle protruding a few inches above the hide of his back-neck. The spectators hoot their contempt for the failure; but with no sign of pity for the beast. The bull is weakened, but trots about and makes a few runs at cloths, and the sword is drawn from his hide by an agile dart-sticker (banderillero), and given to the black bully in dark green, who makes one more lunge, with no better success. The bull runs round, and reels, and staggers, and falls half down, gets partly up, lows and breathes heavily, is pushed over and held down, until a butcher dispatches him with a sharp knife, at the spinal cord. Then come the opened gates, the three horses abreast, decked with ribbons, the hard tug at the bull's body over the ground, his limbs still swaying with remaining life, the clash and clang of the band, and the yells of the people.

Shall I stay another? Perhaps it may be more successful, and—if the new bull will only bruise somebody! But the new bull is a failure. After all their attempts to excite him, he only trots round, and snuffs at the gates; and the cry of "Fuera el toro!" becomes so general, with the significant triple beat of the feet, in time with the words, all over the house, that the gates are opened, and the bull trots through, to his quarters.

But the meanness, and cruelty, and impotency of this crowd! They cry out to the spear-men and the dart-men, and to the tormentors, and to the bull, and to the horses, and to each other, in a Babel of sounds, where no man's voice can possibly be distinguished ten feet from him, all manner of advice and encouragement or derision, like children at a play. One full grown, well-dressed young man, near me, kept up a constant cry to the men in the ring, when I am sure no one could distinguish his words, and no one cared to—until I became so irritated that I could have throttled him.

But, such you are! You can cry and howl at bull-fights and cockfights and in the pits of operas and theaters, and drive bulls and horses distracted, and urge gallant gamecocks to the death, and applaud opera singers into patriotic songs, and leave them to imprisonment and fines—and you yourselves cannot lift a finger, or join hand to hand, or bring to the hazard life, fortune, or honor, for your liberty and your dignity as men. Work your slaves, torture your bulls, fight your gamecocks, crown your dancers and singers—and leave the weightier matters of judgment and justice, of fame by sea and land, of letters and arts and sciences, of private right and public honor, the present and future of your race and of your native land, to the care of others—of a people of no better blood than your own, strangers and sojourners among you!

The next bull is treated to a refinement of torture, in the form of darts filled with heavy China crackers, which explode on the neck of the poor beast. I could not see that even this made him really dangerous. The light-complexioned, green-and-silver matador dispatches him, as he did the first bull, with a single lunge, and—a fall and a quiver, and all is over!

The fifth bull is a failure and is allowed to go out of the ring. The sixth is nearly the same with the others, harmless if let alone, and goaded into short-lived activity, but not into anything like fury or even a dangerous animosity. He is treated to fire-crackers, and gores one horse a little—the horse standing, side on, and taking it, until the bull is driven off by the punching of the spear; and runs at the other horse, and, to my delight, upsets the rider, but unfortunately without hurting him, and the black-haired matador in green tries his hand on him and fails again, and is hooted, and takes to throwing darts, and gets a fall, and looks disconcerted, and gets his sword again, and makes another false thrust; and the crippled and bleeding animal is thrown down and dispatched by the butcher with his short knife, and drawn off by the three poor horses. The gates close, and I hurry out in a din of shouts and drums and trumpets, the great crowd waiting for the last bull—but I have seen enough.

There is no volante waiting, and I have to take my seat in an omnibus, and wait for the end of the scene. The confusion of cries and shouts and the interludes of music still goes on, for a quarter of an hour, and then the crowd begins to pour out, and to scatter over the ground. Four faces in a line are heading for my omnibus. There is no mistaking that head man, the file leader. "Down East" is written legibly all over his face. Tall, thin, sallow, grave, circumspect! The others are not counterparts. They vary. But "New England" is graven on all.

"Wa-a-al!" says the leader, as he gets into the omnibus. No reply. They take their seats, and wipe their foreheads. One expectorates. Another looks too wise for utterance. "By," ... a long pause—How will he end it?—"Jingoes!" That is a failure. It is plain he fell short, and did not end as he intended. The sentiment of the four has not yet got uttered. The fat, flaxen-haired man makes his attempt. "If there is a new milch cow in Vermont that wouldn't show more fight, under such usage, than them bulls, I'd buy her and make a present of her to Governor *Cunchy*—or whatever they call him."

This is practical and direct, and opens the way to a more free interchange. The northern ice is thawed. The meanness and cruelty of the exhibition is commented upon. The moral view is not overlooked, nor underrated.—None but cowards would be so cruel. And last of all, it is an imposition. Their money has been obtained under false pretences. A suit would lie to recover it back; but the poor devils are welcome to the money. The coach fills up with Cubans; and the noise of the pavements drowns the further reflections of the four philanthropists, patriots and economists.

XIX

HAVANA: More Manners and Customs

The people of Cuba have a mode of calling attention by a sound of the tongue and lips, a sort of "P—s—t!" after the fashion of some parts of the continent of Europe. It is universal here; and is used not only to servants and children, but between themselves, and to strangers. It has a mean sound, to us. They make it clear and penetrating; yet it seems a poor, effeminate sibilation, and no generous, open-mouthed call. It is the mode of stopping a volante, calling a waiter, attracting the attention of a friend, or calling the notice of a stranger. I have no doubt, if a fire were to break out at the next door, a Cuban would call "P—s—t!"

They beckon a person to come to them by the reverse of our motion. They raise the open hand, with the palm outwards, bending the fingers toward the person they are calling. We should interpret it to be a sign to go away.

Smoking is universal, and all but constant. I have amused myself, in the street, by seeing what proportion of those I meet have cigars or cigarettes in their mouths. Sometimes it has been one half, sometimes one in three. The cigar is a great leveller. Any man may stop another for a light. I have seen the poor porters, on the wharf, bow to gentlemen, strangers to them, and hold out a cigar, and the gentlemen stop, give a light, and go on—all as of course.

In the evening, called on the Señoritas F——, at the house of Mr. B——, and on the American young lady at Señor M—— 's, and on Mrs. Howe, at Mde. Almy's, to offer to take letters or packets. At Mrs. Almy's, there is a gentleman from New York, Mr. G——, who is dying of consumption. His only wish is to live until the "Cahawba" comes in, that he may at least die at sea, if he cannot survive until she reaches New York. He has a horror of dying here, and being buried in the Potter's Field. Dr. Howe has just come from his chamber.

I drove out to the bishop's, to pay my parting respects. It is about half-past eight in the evening. He has just returned from his evening drive, is dressed in a cool, cambric dressing-gown, after a bath, and is taking a quiet cigar, in his high-roofed parlor. He is very cordial and polite, and talks again about the Thirty Millions Bill, and asks what I think of the result, and what I have seen of the island, and my opinion of the religious and charitable institutions. I praise the Belén and the Sisters of Charity, and condemn the prison, and he appears to agree with me. He appreciates the learning and zeal of the Brothers of Belén; speaks in the highest terms of the devotedness of the Sisters of Charity; and admits the great faults of the prison, but says it was built recently, at an enormous out lay, and he supposes the government is reluctant to be at the expense of abandoning it and building another. He charges me with messages of remembrance and respect to acquaintances we have in common. As I take my leave, he goes with me to the outer gate, which is kept locked, and again takes leave, for two leave-takings are the custom of the country, and returns to the solitude of his house.

Yesterday I drove out to the Cerro, to see the coolie jail, or market, where the imported coolies are kept for sale. It is a well-known place, and open to all visitors. The building has a fair-looking front; and through this I enter, past two porters, into an open yard in the rear, where, on the gravel ground, are squatting a double line of coolies, with heads shaved, except a tuft on the crown, dressed in loose Chinese garments of blue and yellow. The dealer, who is a calm, shrewd, heartless-looking man, speaking English as well as if it were his native tongue, comes out with me, calls to the coolies, and they all stand up in a double line, facing inward, and we pass through them, preceded by a driver armed with the usual badge of the plantation driver, the short, limber whip. The dealer does not hesitate to tell me the terms on which the contracts are made, as the trade is not illegal. His account is this—The importer receives $340 for each coolie, and the purchaser agrees to pay the coolie four dollars per month, and to give him food, and two suits of clothes a year. For this, he has his services for eight years. The contract is reduced to writing before a magistrate, and two originals are made, one kept by the coolie and one by the purchaser, and each in Chinese and Spanish.

This was a strange and striking exhibition of power. Two or three white men, bringing hundreds of Chinese thousands of miles, to a new climate and people, holding them prisoners, selling their services to masters having an unknown tongue and an unknown religion, to work at unknown trades, for inscrutable purposes!

The coolies did not look unhealthy, though some had complaints of the eyes; yet they looked, or I fancied they looked, some of them, unhappy, and some of them stolid. One I am sure had the leprosy although the dealer would not admit it. The dealer did not deny their tendency to suicide, and the danger of attempting to chastise them, but alleged their great superiority to the Negro in intelligence, and contended that their condition was good, and better than in China, having four dollars a month, and being free at the end of eight years. He said, which I found to be true, that after being separated and employed in work, they let their hair grow, and adopt the habits and dress of the country. The newly-arrived coolies wear tufts, and blue-and-yellow, loose, Chinese clothes. Those who have been here long are distinguishable from the whites only by the peculiar tinge of the cheek, and the form of the eye. The only respect in which his account differed from what I heard elsewhere was in the amount the importer receives, which has always been stated to me at $400. While I am talking with him, a gentleman comes and passes down the line. He is probably a purchaser, I judge; and I leave my informant to follow what is more for his interest than talking with me.

The importation has not yet existed eight years. So the question, what will become of these men, exotics, without women or children, taking no root in the land, has not come to a solution. The constant question is—will they remain and mix with the other races? Will they be permitted to remain? Will they be able to go back? In 1853, they were not noticed in the census; and in 1857, hardly noticed. The number imported may, to some extent, be obtained from the records and files of the aduana, but not so as to be relied upon. I heard the number estimated at 200,000 by intelligent and well-informed Cubans. Others put it as low as 60,000. Certain it is that coolies are to be met with everywhere, in town and country.

So far as I can learn, there is no law in China regulating the contracts and shipment of Chinese coolies, and none in Cuba regulating their transportation, landing, or treatment while here. The trade has grown up and been permitted and recognized, but not regulated. It is yet to be determined how far the contract is enforceable against either party. Those coolies that are taken from the British East Indies to British islands are taken under contracts, with regulations, as to their exportation and return, understood and enforced. Not so the Chinese coolies. Their importers are *lege soluti*. Some say the government will insist on their being returned. But the prevailing impression is that they will be brought in debt, and bound over again for their debts, or in some other way secured to a life-long servitude.

Mr.———, a very wealthy and intelligent planter, tells me he is to go over to Regla, to-morrow morning, to see a lot of slaves offered for sale to him, and asks me if I have ever seen a sale of slaves. I never have seen that sight, and accept his invitation. We are to leave here at half-past six, or seven, at the latest. All work is early here; I believe I have mentioned that the hour of 'Change for merchants is 7.30 A.M.

XX

HAVANA: Slaves, Lotteries, Cockfights and Filibusters

Rise early, and walk to the sea-baths, and take a delightful float and swim. And refreshing it is, after a feverish night in my hot room, where I did not sleep an hour all night, but heard every quarter-hour struck, and the boatswain's whistle of the watchmen and their full cry of the hour and the weather, at every clock-strike. From the bath, I look out over the wall, far to the northeast, in the hope of catching a glimpse of the "Cahawba's" smoke. This is the day of her expected arrival. My New York friends and myself feel that we have seen Havana to our satisfaction, and the heat is becoming intense. We are beginning to receive advice against eating fruit after *café au lait*, or bananas with wine, and in favor of high-crowned hats at noon to prevent congestion from heat, and to avoid fogs in the morning. But there is no "Cahawba" in sight, and I hear only the bray of trumpets and roll of drums from the Morro and Cabaña and Punta, and the clanking march of the chain-gang down the Paseo, and the march of the guard to trumpet and drum.

Mr.—— is punctual at seven, his son with him, and a man in a suit of white linen, who is the broker employed by Mr.——. We take a ferry-boat and cross to the Regla; and a few minutes' walk brings us to a small nail factory, where all the workmen are coolies. In the back-yard of this factory is a line of low buildings, from which the slaves are brought out, to be shown. We had taken up, at the ferry-boat, a small, thin, sharp-faced man, who was the dealer. The slaves are formed in a semicircle, by the dealer and broker. The broker pushed and pulled them about in a coarse, careless manner, worse than the manner of the dealer. I am glad he is not to be their master. Mr.—— spoke kindly to them. They were fully dressed; and no examination was made except by the eye; and no exhibitions of strength or agility were required, and none of those offensive examinations of which we read so much. What examination had been made or was to be made by the broker, out of my presence, I do not know. The "lot" consisted of about fifty, of both sexes and of all ages, some being old, and some very young. They were not a valuable lot, and Mr.—— refused to purchase them all. The dealer offered to separate them. Mr.—— selected about half of them, and they were set apart. I watched the countenances of all—the taken and the left. It was hard to decipher the character of their emotions. A kind of fixed hopelessness marked the faces of some, listlessness that of others, and others seemed anxious or disappointed, but whether because taken or rejected, it was hard to say. When the separation was made, and they knew its purpose, still no complaint was made and no suggestion ventured by the slaves that a tie of nature or affection was broken. I asked Mr.—— if some of them might not be related. He said he should attend to that, as he never separated families. He spoke to each of those he had chosen, separately, and asked if they had parent or child, husband or wife, or brother or sister among those who were rejected. A few pointed out their relations, and Mr.—— took them into his lot. One was an aged mother, one a wife, and another a little daughter. I am satisfied that no separations were made in this case, and equally satisfied that neither the dealer nor the broker would have asked the question.

I asked Mr.—— on what principle he made his selection, as he did not seem to me always to take the strongest. "On the principle of race," said he. He told me that these Negroes were probably natives of Africa, bozales, except the youngest, and that the signs of the races were known to all planters. A certain race he named as having always more intelligence and ambition than any other; as more difficult to manage, but far superior when well managed. All of this race in the company, he took at once, whatever their age or strength. I think the preferred tribe was the Lucumí, but am not certain.

From this place, I made a short visit to the almacén de azúcar, in the Regla, the great storehouses of sugar. These are a range of one-story, stone warehouses, so large that a great part of the sugar crop of the island, as I am told, could be stored in them. Here the vessels go to load, and the merchants store their sugar here, as wine is stored in the London docks.

The Cubans are careful of the diet of foreigners, even in winter. I bought a couple of oranges, and young Mr.—— bought a sapote, a kind of sweet-sour apple, when the broker said "Take care! Did you not have milk with your coffee?" I inquired, and they told me it was not well to eat fresh fruit soon after taking milk, or to take bananas with wine, or to drink spirits. "But is this in winter, also?" "Yes; and it is already very hot, and there is danger of fever among strangers."

Went to La Dominica, the great restaurant and depot of preserves and sweetmeats for Havana, and made out my order for preserves to take home with me. After consultation, I am advised to make up my list as follows: guava of Peru, limes, mamey apples, soursop, coconut, oranges, guava jelly, guava marmalade, and almonds.

The ladies tell me there is a kind of fine linen sold here, called bolan, which it is difficult to obtain in the United States, and which would be very proper to take home for a present. On this advice, I bought a quantity of it, of blue and white, at La Diana, a shop on the corner of Calle de Obispo and San Ignacio.

Breakfasted with a wealthy and intelligent gentleman, a large planter, who is a native of Cuba, but of European descent. A very nice breakfast, of Spanish mixed dishes, rice cooked to perfection, fruits, claret, and the only cup of good black tea I have tasted in Cuba. At Le Grand's, we have no tea but the green.

At breakfast, we talked freely on the subject of the condition and prospects of Cuba; and I obtained from my host his views of the economic and industrial situation of the island. He was confident that the number of slaves does not exceed 500,000, to 200,000 free blacks, and 600,000 or 700,000 whites. His argument led him to put the number of slaves as low as he could, yet he estimated it far above that of the census of 1857, which makes it 375,000. But no one regards the census of slaves as correct. There is a tax on slaves, and the government has little chance of getting them stated at the full number. One planter said to a friend of mine, a year or two ago, that his two hundred slaves were returned as one hundred. I find the best opinions put the slaves at 650,000, the free blacks at 200,000, and the whites at 700,000.

Havana is flooded with lottery-ticket vendors. They infest every eating-house and public way, and vex you at dinner, in your walks and rides. They sell for one grand lottery, established and guaranteed by the government, always in operation, and yielding to the state a net revenue of nearly two millions a year. The Cubans are infatuated with this lottery. All classes seem to embark in it. Its effect is especially bad on the slaves, who invest in it all they can earn, beg, or steal, allured by the glorious vision of possibly purchasing their freedom, and elevating themselves into the class of proprietors.

Some gentlemen at Le Grand's have been to a cock-fight. I shall be obliged to leave the island without seeing this national sport for which every town, and every village has a pit, a Valle de Gallos. They tell me it was a very exciting scene among the spectators. Negroes, free and slave, low whites, coolies, and men of high condition were all frantically betting. Most of the bets were made by holding up the fingers and by other signs, between boxes and galleries. They say I should hardly credit the large sums which the most ordinary looking men staked and paid.

I am surprised to find what an impression the López expedition made in Cuba—a far greater impression than is commonly supposed in the United States. The fears of the government and hopes of sympathizers exaggerated the force, and the whole military power of the government was stirred against them. Their little force of a few hundred broken-down men and lads, deceived and deserted, fought a body of eight times their number, and kept them at bay, causing great slaughter. The railroad trains brought the wounded into Havana, car after car; rumors of defeat filled the city; artillery was sent out; and the actual loss of the Spaniards, in killed and wounded, was surprisingly large. On the front wall of the Cabaña, plainly seen from the deck of every vessel that leaves or enters the port, is a monument to the honor of those who fell in the battle with the filibusteros. The spot where López was garroted, in front of the Punta, is pointed out, as well as the slope of the hill from the castle of Atares, where his surviving followers were shot.

XXI

A SUMMING-UP: Society, Politics, Religion, Slavery, Resources and Reflections

To an American, from the free states, Cuba presents an object of singular interest. His mind is occupied and almost oppressed by the thought of the strange problems that are in process of solution around him. He is constantly a critic, and a philosophizer, if not a philosopher. A despotic civil government, compulsory religious uniformity, and slavery are in full possession of the field. He is always seeking information as to causes, processes and effects, and almost as constantly baffled. There are three classes of persons in Cuba, from whom he receives contradictory and irreconcilable statements: the Cubans, the Spaniards, and foreigners of other nations. By Cubans, I mean the Criollos (Creoles), or natives of Cuba. By Spaniards, I mean the Peninsulares, or natives of Old Spain. In the third class are comprised the Americans, English, French, Germans, and all other foreigners, except Spaniards, who are residents on the island, but not natives. This last class is large, possesses a great deal of wealth, and includes a great number of merchants, bankers and other traders.

The Spaniards, or Peninsulares, constitute the army and navy, the officers of the government in all departments, judicial, educational, fiscal and postal, the revenue and the police, the upper clergy, and a large and wealthy class of merchants, bankers, shopkeepers, and mechanics. The higher military and civil officers are from all parts of Spain; but the Catalans furnish the great body of the mechanics and small traders. The Spaniards may be counted on as opponents of the independence of Cuba, and especially of her annexation to the United States. In their political opinions, they vary. Some belong to the liberal, or Progresista party, and others are advocates of, or at least apologists for, the present order of things. Their force and influence is increased by the fact that the government encourages its military and civil officers, at the expiration of their terms of service, to remain in the island, still holding some nominal office, or on the pay of a retired list.

The foreign residents, not Spaniards, are chiefly engaged in commerce, banking, or trade, or are in scientific or mechanic employments. These do not intend to become citizens of Cuba. They strike no root into the soil, but feel that they are only sojourners, for purposes of their own. Of all classes of persons, I know of none whose situation is more unfavorable to the growth and development of sentiments of patriotism and philanthropy, and of interest in the future of a race, than foreigners, temporarily resident, for purposes of money-making only, in a country with which they have nothing in common, in the future or the past. This class is often called impartial. I do not agree to that use of the term. They are, indeed, free from the bias of feeling or sentiment; and from the bias generated by the combined action of men thinking and feeling alike, which we call political party. But they are subject to the attractions of interest; and interest will magnetize the mind as effectually as feeling. Planted in a soil where the more tender and delicate fibers can take no hold, they stand by the strong tap-root of interest. It is for their immediate advantage to preserve peace and the existing order of things; and even if it may be fairly argued that their ultimate interests would be benefited by a change, yet the process is hazardous, and the result not sure; and, at most, they would do no more than take advantage of the change, if it occurred. I should say, as a general thing, that this class is content with the present order of things. The island is rich, production is large, commerce flourishes, life and property are well protected, and if a man does not concern himself with political or religious questions, he has nothing to fear. Of the Americans in this class, many, doubtless, may be favorably inclined toward annexation, but they are careful talkers, if they are so; and the foreigners, not Americans, are of course earnestly opposed to it, and the pendency of the question tends to draw them towards the present government.

It remains only to speak of the Cubans. They are commonly styled Creoles. But as that word includes natives of all Spanish America, it is not quite definite. Of the Cubans, a few are advocates of the present government— but very few. The far greater part are disaffected. They desire something approximating to self-government. If that can be had from Spain, they would prefer it. If not, there is nothing for them but independence, or annexation to some other power. Not one of them thinks of independence; and if it be annexation, I believe their present impulse is toward the United States. Yet on this point, among even the most disaffected of the Cubans, there is a difference of opinion. Many of them are sincere emancipationists, and fear that if they come in at the southern end of our Union, that question is closed for ever. Others fear that the Anglo-Saxon race would swallow up the power and property of the island, as they have done in California and Texas, and that the Creoles would go to the wall.

It has been my fortune to see persons of influence and intelligence from each of these chief divisions, and from the subdivisions, and to talk with them freely. From the sum of their conflicting opinions and conflicting statements, I have endeavored to settle upon some things as certain; and, as to other things, to ascertain how far the debatable ground extends, and the principles which govern the debate. From all these sources, and from my own observations, I will endeavor to set down what I think to be the present state of Cuba, in its various interesting features, trusting to do it as becomes one whose acquaintance with the island has been so recent and so short.

POLITICAL CONDITION

When the liberal constitutions were in force in Spain, in the early part of this century, the benefits of them extended to Cuba. Something like a provincial legislature was established; juntas, or advisory boards and committees, discussed public questions, and made recommendations; a militia was organized; the right to bear arms was recognized; tribunals, with something of the nature of juries, passed upon certain questions; the press was free, and Cuba sent delegates to the Spanish Cortes. This state of things continued, with but few interruptions or variations, to 1825.

Then was issued the celebrated Royal Order of May 29, 1825, under which Cuba has been governed to the present hour. This Royal Order is the only constitution of Cuba. It was probably intended merely as a temporary order to the then Captain-General; but it has been found convenient to adhere to it. It clothes the Captain-General with the fullest powers, the tests and limit of which are as follows: " ... fully investing you with the whole extent of power which, by the royal ordinances, is granted to the governors of besieged towns. In consequence thereof, His Majesty most amply and unrestrictedly authorizes your Excellency not only to remove from the island such persons, holding offices from government or not, whatever their occupation, rank, class, or situation in life may be, whose residence there you may believe prejudicial, or whose public or private conduct may appear suspicious to you...." Since 1825, Cuba has been not only under martial law, but in a state of siege.

As to the more or less of justice or injustice, of honesty or peculation, of fidelity or corruption, of liberality or severity, with which these powers may have been exercised, a residence of a few days, the reading of a few books, and conversations with a few men, though on both sides, give me no right to pronounce. Of the probabilities, all can judge, especially when we remember that these powers are wielded by natives of one country over natives of another country.

Since 1825, there has been no legislative assembly in Cuba, either provincial or municipal. The municipal corporations (ayuntamientos) were formerly hereditary, the dignity was purchasable, and no doubt the bodies were corrupt. But they exercised some control, at least in the levying and expending of taxes; and, being hereditary, were somewhat independent, and might have served, like those of Europe in the middle ages, as nuclei of popular liberties. These have lost the few powers they possessed, and the members are now mere appointees of the Captain-General. Since 1836, Cuba has been deprived of its right to a delegation in the Cortes. Since 1825, vestiges of anything approaching to popular assemblies, juntas, a jury, independent tribunals, a right of voting, or a right to bear arms, have vanished from the island. The press is under censorship; and so are the theaters and operas. When "I Puritani" is played, the singers are required to substitute Lealtad for Libertad, and one singer was fined and imprisoned for recusancy; and Facciolo, the printer of a secretly circulated newspaper, advocating the cause of Cuban independence, was garroted. The power of banishing, without a charge made, or a trial, or even a record, but on the mere will of the Captain-General, persons whose presence he thinks, or professes to think, prejudicial to the government, whatever their condition, rank, or office, has been frequently exercised, and hangs at all hours over the head of every Cuban. Besides, that terrible power which is restrained only by the analogy of a state of siege, may be at any time called into action. Cubans may be, and I suppose usually are, regularly charged and tried before judges, on political accusations; but this is not their right; and the judges themselves, even of the highest court, the Real Audiencia, may be deposed and banished, at the will of the military chief.

According to the strictness of the written law, no native Cuban can hold any office of honor, trust, or emolument in Cuba. The army and navy are composed of Spaniards, even to the soldiers in the ranks, and to the sailors at the guns. It is said by the supporters of the government that this order is not adhered to; and they point to a capitán-general, an intendente, and a chief of the customs, who were Cubans. Still, such is the written law; and if a few Cubans are put into office against the law, those who are so favored are likely to be the most servile of officers, and the situation of the rest is only the more degraded. Notwithstanding the exceptions, it may be said with substantial truth that an independent Cuban has open to him no career, civil or military. There is a force of volunteers, to which some Cubans are admitted, but they hold their places at the will of the government; and none are allowed to join or remain with them unless they are acceptable to the government.

There are vexatious and mortifying regulations, too numerous and minute to be complied with or even remembered, and which put the people in danger of fines or extortion at every turn. Take, for instance, the regulation that no man shall entertain a stranger over night at his house, without previous notice to the magistrate. As to the absolute prohibition of concealed weapons, and of all weapons but the regulation sword and pistols—it was no doubt introduced and enforced by Tacón as a means of suppressing assassinations, broils and open violence; and it has made life safer in Havana than it is in New York; yet it cannot be denied that it created a serious disability. In fine, what is the Spanish government in Cuba but an armed monarchy, encamped in the midst of a disarmed and disfranchised people?

The taxes paid by the Cubans on their property, and the duties levied on their commerce, are enormous, making a net income of not less than $16,000,000 a year. Cuba pays all the expenses of its own government, the salaries of all officers, the entire cost of the army and navy quartered upon it, the maintenance of the Roman Catholic religion, and of all the charitable and benevolent institutions, and sends an annual remittance to Spain.

The number of Spanish men-of-war stationed on the coast, varies from twenty-five to thirty. Of the number of soldiers of the regular army in Cuba, it is difficult to form an opinion. The official journal puts them at 30,000. The lowest estimate I heard, was 25,000; and the highest was 40,000. Judging from the number of sick I saw at the Hospital Militar, I should not be surprised if the larger estimate was nearer the truth.

But details are of little importance. The actual administration may be a little more or less rigid or lax. In its legal character, the government is an unmixed despotism of one nation over another.

RELIGION

No religion is tolerated but the Roman Catholic. Formerly the church was wealthy, authoritative and independent, and checked the civil and military power by an ecclesiastical power wielded also by the dominant nation. But the property of the church has been sequestrated and confiscated, and the government now owns all the property once ecclesiastical, including the church edifices, and appoints all the clergy, from the bishop to the humblest country curate. All are salaried officers. And so powerless is the church, that, however scandalous may be the life of a parish priest, the bishop cannot remove him. He can only institute proceedings against him before a tribunal over which the government has large control, with a certainty of long delays and entire uncertainty as to the result. The bishopric of Havana was formerly one of the wealthiest sees in Christendom. Now the salary is hardly sufficient to meet the demands which custom makes in respect of charity, hospitality and style of living. It may be said, I think with truth, that the Roman Catholic Church has now neither civil nor political power in Cuba.

That there was a long period of time during which the morals of the clergy were excessively corrupt, I think there can be no doubt. Make every allowance for theological bias, or for irreligious bias, in the writers and tourists in Cuba, still, the testimony from Roman Catholics themselves is irresistible. The details, it is not worth while to contend about. It is said that a family of children, with a recognized relation to its female head, which the rule of celibacy prevented ever becoming a marriage, was general with the country priesthood. A priest who was faithful to that relation, and kept from cockfighting and gambling, was esteemed a respectable man by the common people. Cuba became a kind of Botany Bay for the Romish clergy. There they seem to have been concealed from the eye of discipline. With this state of things, there existed, naturally enough, a vast amount of practical infidelity among the people, and especially among the men, who, it is said, scarcely recognized religious obligations at all.

No one can observe the state of Europe now, without seeing that the rapidity of communication by steam and electricity has tended to add to the efficiency of the central power of the Roman Catholic Church, and to the efficacy and extent of its discipline. Cuba has begun to feel these effects. Whether they have yet reached the interior, or the towns generally, I do not know; but the concurrent testimony of all classes satisfied me that a considerable change has been effected in Havana. The instrumentalities which that church brings to bear in such cases, are in operation: frequent preaching, and stricter discipline of confession and communion. The most marked result is in the number of men, and men of character and weight, who have become earnest in the use of these means. Much of this must be attributed, no doubt, to the Jesuits; but how long they will be permitted to remain here, and what will be the permanent effects of the movement, I cannot, of course, conjecture.

I do not enter into the old field of contest. "We care not," says one side, "which be cause and which effect;—whether the people are Papists, because they are what they are, or are as they are because they are Papists. It is enough that the two things coexist." The other side replies that no Protestant institutions have ever yet been tried for any length of time, and to any large extent, with southern races, in a tropical climate; and the question—what would be their influence, and what the effect of surrounding causes upon them, lies altogether in the region of conjecture, or, at best, of faith.

Of the moral habits of the clergy, as of the people, at the present time, I am entirely unable to judge. I saw very little that indicated the existence of any vices whatever among the people. Five minutes of a street view of London by night, exhibits more vice, to the casual observer, than all Havana for a year. I do not mean to say that the social morals of the Cubans are good, or are bad; I only mean to say that I am not a judge of the question.

The most striking indication of the want of religious control is the disregard of the Lord's Day. All business seems to go on as usual, unless it be in the public offices. The chain-gang works in the streets, under public officers. House-building and mechanic trades go on uninterrupted; and the shops are more active than ever. The churches, to be sure, are open and well filled in the morning; and I do not refer to amusements and recreations; I speak of public, secular labor. The Church must be held to some responsibility for this. Granted that Sunday is not the Sabbath. Yet, it is a day which, by the rule of the Roman Church, the English Church in England and America, the Greek Church and other Oriental Churches—all claiming to rest the rule on Apostolic authority, as well as by the usage of Protestants on the continent of Europe—whether Lutherans or Calvinists—is a day of rest from secular labor, and especially from enforced labor. Pressing this upon an intelligent ecclesiastic, his reply to me was that the Church could not enforce the observance—that it must be enforced by the civil authorities; and the civil authorities fall in with the selfishness and gratifications of the ruling classes. And he appealed to the change lately wrought in Paris, in these respects, as evidence of the consistency of his Church. This is an answer, so far as concerns the Church's direct authority; but it is an admission either of feeble moral power, or of neglect of duty in times past. An embarrassment in the way of more strictness as to secular labor, arises from the fact that slaves are entitled to their time on Sundays, beyond the necessary labor of providing for the day; and this time they may use in working out their freedom.

Another of the difficulties the church has to contend with, arises out of Negro slavery. The Church recognizes the unity of all races, and allows marriage between them. The civil law of Cuba, under the interpretations in force here, prohibits marriage between whites and persons who have any tinge of the black blood. In consequence of this rule, concubinage prevails, to a great extent, between whites and mulattoes or quadroons, often with recognition of the children. If either party to this arrangement comes under the influence of the Church's discipline, the relation must terminate. The Church would allow and advise marriage; but the law prohibits it—and if there should be a separation, there may be no provision for the children. This state of things creates no small obstacle to the influence of the Church over the domestic relations.

SLAVERY

It is difficult to come to a satisfactory conclusion as to the number of slaves in Cuba. The census of 1857 puts it at 375,000; but neither this census nor that of 1853 is to be relied upon, on this point. The Cubans are taxed for their slaves, and the government find it difficult, as I have said, to get correct returns. No person of intelligence in Cuba, however desirous to put the number at the lowest, has stated it to me at less than 500,000. Many set it at 700,000. I am inclined to think that 600,000 is the nearest to the truth.

The census makes the free blacks, in 1857, 125,000. It is thought to be 200,000, by the best authorities. The whites are about 700,000. The only point in which the census seems to agree with public opinion, is in the proportion. Both make the proportion of blacks to be about one free black to three slaves; and make the whites not quite equal to the entire number of blacks, free and slave together.

To ascertain the condition of slaves in Cuba, two things are to be considered: first, the laws, and secondly, the execution of the laws. The written laws, there is no great difficulty in ascertaining. As to their execution, there is room for opinion. At this point, one general remark should be made, which I deem to be of considerable importance. The laws relating to slavery do not emanate from the slave-holding mind; nor are they interpreted or executed by the slave-holding class. The slave benefits by the division of power and property between the two rival and even hostile races of whites, the Creoles and the Spaniards. Spain is not slave-holding, at home; and so long as the laws are made in Spain, and the civil offices are held by Spaniards only, the slave has at least the advantage of a conflict of interests and principles, between the two classes that are concerned in his bondage.

The fact that one Negro in every four is free, indicates that the laws favor emancipation. They do both favor emancipation, and favor the free blacks after emancipation. The stranger visiting Havana will see a regiment of one thousand free black volunteers, parading with the troops of the line and the white volunteers, and keeping guard in the Obra Pia. When it is remembered that the bearing arms and performing military duty as volunteers is esteemed an honor and privilege, and is not allowed to the whites of Creole birth, except to a few who are favored by the government, the significance of this fact may be appreciated. The Cuban slave-holders are more impatient under this favoring of the free blacks than under almost any other act of the government. They see in it an attempt, on the part of the authorities, to secure the sympathy and coöperation of the free blacks, in case of a revolutionary movement—to set race against race, and to make the free blacks familiar with military duty, while the whites are growing up in ignorance of it. In point of civil privileges, the free blacks are the equals of the whites. In courts of law, as witnesses or parties, no difference is known; and they have the same rights as to the holding of lands and other property. As to their social position, I have not the means of speaking. I should think it quite as good as it is in New England, if not better.

So far as to the position of the blacks, when free. The laws also directly favor emancipation. Every slave has a right to go to a magistrate and have himself valued, and on paying the valuation, to receive his free papers. The valuation is made by three assessors, of whom the master nominates one and the magistrate the other two. The slave is not obliged to pay the entire valuation at once; but may pay it in installments, of not less than fifty dollars each. These payments are not made as mere advances of money, on the security of the master's receipt, but are part purchases. Each payment makes the slave an owner of such a portion of himself, *pro parte indivisa*, or as the common law would say, in tenancy-in-common, with his master. If the valuation be one thousand dollars, and he pays one hundred dollars, he is owned, one-tenth by himself and nine-tenths by his master. It has been said, in nearly all the American books on Cuba, that, on paying a share, he becomes entitled to a corresponding share of his time and labor; but, from the best information I can get, I think this is a mistake. The payment affects the proprietary title, but not the usufruct. Until all is paid, the master's dominion over the slave is not reduced, as respects either discipline, or labor, or right of transfer; but if the slave is sold, or goes by operation of law to heirs or legatees or creditors, they take only the interest not paid for, subject to the right of future payment under the valuation.

There is another provision, which, at first sight, may not appear very important, but which is, I am inclined to think, the best practical protection the slave has against ill-treatment by his master: that is, the right to a compulsory sale. A slave may, on the same process of valuation compel his master to transfer him to any person who will pay the money. For this purpose, he need establish no cause of complaint. It is enough if he desires to be transferred, and some one is willing to buy him. This operates as a check upon the master, and an inducement to him to remove special causes of dissatisfaction; and it enables the better class of slave-holders in a neighborhood, if cases of ill-usage are known, to relieve the slave, without contention or pecuniary loss.

In making the valuation, whether for emancipation or compulsory transfer, the slave is to be estimated at his value as a common laborer, according to his strength, age, and health. If he knows an art or trade, however much that may add to his value, only one hundred dollars can be added to the estimate for this trade or art. Thus the skill, industry and character of the slave, do not furnish an obstacle to his emancipation or transfer. On the contrary, all that his trade or art adds to his value, above one hundred dollars, is, in fact, a capital for his benefit.

There are other provisions for the relief of the slave, which, although they may make even a better show on paper, are of less practical value. On complaint and proof of cruel treatment, the law will dissolve the relation between master and slave. No slave can be flogged with more than twenty-five lashes, by the master's authority. If his offence is thought greater than that punishment will suffice for, the public authorities must be called in. A slave mother may buy the freedom of her infant, for twenty-five dollars. If slaves have been married by the Church, they cannot be separated against their will; and the mother has the right to keep her nursing child. Each slave is entitled to his time on Sundays and all other holidays, beyond two hours allowed for necessary labor, except on sugar estates during the grinding season. Every slave born on the island is to be baptized and instructed in the Catholic faith, and to receive Christian burial. Formerly, there were provisions requiring religious services and instruction on each plantation, according to its size; but I believe these are either repealed, or become a dead letter. There are also provisions respecting the food, clothing and treatment of slaves in other respects, and the providing of a sick room and medicines, &c.; and the government has appointed magistrates, styled síndicos, numerous enough, and living in all localities, whose duty it is to attend to the petitions and complaints of slaves, and to the measures relating to their sale, transfer or emancipation.

As to the enforcement of these laws, I have little or no personal knowledge to offer; but some things, I think, I may treat as reasonably sure, from my own observation, and from the concurrent testimony of books, and of persons of all classes with whom I have conversed.

The rule respecting religion is so far observed as this, that infants are baptized, and all receive Christian burial. But there is no enforcement of the obligation to give the slaves religious instruction, or to allow them to attend public religious service. Most of those in the rural districts see no church and no priest, from baptism to burial. If they do receive religious instruction, or have religious services provided for them, it is the free gift of the master.

Marriage by the Church is seldom celebrated. As in the Roman Church marriage is a sacrament and indissoluble, it entails great inconvenience upon the master, as regards sales or mortgages, and is a restraint on the Negroes themselves, to which it is not always easy to reconcile them. Consequently, marriages are usually performed by the master only, and of course, carry with them no legal rights or duties. Even this imperfect and dissoluble connection has been but little attended to. While the slave-trade was allowed, the planters supplied their stock with bozales (native Africans) and paid little attention, even on economic principles, to the improvement, or, speaking after the fashion of cattle-farms, to the increase of stock on the plantation. Now that importation is more difficult, and labor is in demand, their attention is more turned to their own stock, and they are beginning to learn, in the physiology of increase, that canon which the Everlasting has fixed against promiscuous intercourse.

The laws respecting valuation, the purchase of freedom at once or by instalments, and the compulsory transfer, I know to be in active operation in the towns, and on plantations affording easy access to towns or magistrates. I heard frequent complaints from slave-holders and those who sympathized with them, as to the operation of these provisions. A lady in Havana had a slave who was an excellent cook; and she had been offered $1700 for him, and refused it. He applied for valuation for the purpose of transfer, and was valued at $1000 as a laborer, which, with the $100 for his trade, made a loss to the owner of $600, and, as no slave can be subsequently sold for a larger sum than his valuation, this provision gave the slave a capital of $600. Another instance was of a planter near Matanzas, who had a slave taught as a carpenter; but after learning his trade, the slave got himself transferred to a master in the city, for the opportunity of working out his freedom, on holidays and in extra hours. So general is the enforcement of these provisions that it is said to have resulted in a refusal of many masters to teach their slaves any art or trade, and in the hiring of the labor of artisans of all sorts, and the confining of the slaves to mere manual labor. I heard of complaints of the conduct of individuals who were charged with attempting to influence the credulous and too ready slaves to agree to be transferred to them, either to gratify some ill-will against the owner, or for some supposed selfish interest. From the frequency of this tone of complaint and anecdote, as well as from positive assertions on good authority, I believe these provisions to have considerable efficacy.

As to the practical advantage the slaves can get from these provisions in remote places; and as to the amount of protection they get anywhere from the special provisions respecting punishment, food, clothing, and treatment generally, almost everything lies in the region of opinion. There is no end to statement and anecdote on each side. If one cannot get a full and lengthened personal experience, not only as the guest of the slave-holder, but as the companion of the local magistrates, of the lower officers on the plantation, of slave-dealers and slave-hunters, and of the emancipated slaves, I advise him to shut his ears to mere anecdotes and general statements, and to trust to reasonable deductions from established facts. The established facts are, that one race, having all power in its hands, holds an inferior race in slavery; that this bondage exists in cities, in populous neighborhoods, and in remote districts; that the owners are human beings, of tropical races, and the slaves are human beings just emerging from barbarism, and that no small part of this power is exercised by a low-lived and low-minded class of intermediate agents. What is likely to be the effect on all the parties to this system, judging from all we know of human nature?

If persons coming from the North are credulous enough to suppose that they will see chains and stripes and tracks of blood; and if, taking letters to the best class of slave-holders, seeing their way of life, and hearing their dinner-table anecdotes, and the breakfast-table talk of the ladies, they find no outward signs of violence or corruption, they will probably, also, be credulous enough to suppose they have seen the whole of slavery. They do not know that that large plantation, with its smoking chimneys, about which they hear nothing, and which their host does not visit, has passed to the creditors of the late owner, who is a bankrupt, and is in charge of a manager, who is to get all he can from it in the shortest time, and to sell off the slaves as he can, having no interest, moral or pecuniary, in their future. They do not know that that other plantation, belonging to the young man who spends half his time in Havana, is an abode of licentiousness and cruelty. Neither do they know that the tall hounds chained at the kennel of the house they are visiting are Cuban bloodhounds, trained to track and to seize. They do not know that the barking last night was a pursuit and capture, in which all the white men on the place took part; and that, for the week past, the men of the plantation have been a committee of detective and protective police. They do not know that the ill-looking man who was there yesterday, and whom the ladies did not like, and all treated with ill-disguised aversion, is a professed hunter of slaves. They have never seen or heard of the Sierra del Cristal, the mountain-range at the eastern end of Cuba, inhabited by runaways, where white men hardly dare to go. Nor do they know that those young ladies, when little children, were taken to the city in the time of the insurrection in the Vuelta de Arriba. They have not heard the story of that downcast-looking girl, the now incorrigibly malignant Negro, and the lying mayoral. In the cities, they are amused by the flashy dresses, indolence and good-humor of the slaves, and pleased with the respectfulness of their manners, and hear anecdotes of their attachment to their masters, and how they so dote upon slavery that nothing but bad advice can entice them into freedom; and are told, too, of the worse condition of the free blacks. They have not visited the slave-jails, or the whipping-posts in the house outside the walls, where low whites do the flogging of the city house-servants, men and women, at so many reals a head.

But the reflecting mind soon tires of the anecdotes of injustice, cruelty and licentiousness on the one hand, and of justice, kindness and mutual attachment, on the other. You know that all coexist; but in what proportion you can only conjecture. You know what slavery must be, in its effect on both the parties to it. You seek to grapple with the problem itself. And, stating it fairly, it is this—Shall the industry of Cuba go on, or shall the island be abandoned to a state of nature? If the former, and if the whites cannot do the hard labor in that climate, and the blacks can, will the seven hundred thousand whites, who own all the land and improvements, surrender them to the blacks and leave the island, or will they remain? If they must be expected to remain, what is to be the relation of the two races? The blacks must do the hard work, or it will not be done. Shall it be the enforced labor of slavery, or shall the experiment of free labor be tried? Will the government try the experiment, and if so, on what terms and in what manner? If something is not done by the government, slavery will continue; for a successful insurrection of slaves in Cuba is impossible, and manumissions do not gain upon the births and importations.

MATERIAL RESOURCES AND EDUCATION

Cuba contains more good harbors than does any part of the United States south of Norfolk. Its soil is very rich, and there are no large wastes of sand, either by the sea or in the interior. The coral rocks bound the sea, and the grass and trees come down to the coral rocks. The surface of the country is diversified by mountains, hills and undulating lands, and is very well wooded, and tolerably well watered. It is interesting and picturesque to the eye, and abounds in flowers, trees of all varieties, and birds of rich plumage, though not of rich notes. It has mines of copper, and probably of iron, and is not cursed with gold or silver ore. There is no anthracite, but probably a large amount of a very soft, bituminous coal, which can be used for manufactures.

It has also marble, and other kinds of stone; and the hard woods, as mahogany, cedar, ebony, iron-wood, lignum vitæ, &c., are in abundance. Mineral salt is to be found, and probably in sufficient quantities for the use of the island. It is the boast of the Cubans that the island has no wild beasts or venomous reptiles. This has been so often repeated by tourists and historians that I suppose it must be admitted to be true, with the qualification that they have the scorpion, and tarantula, and nigua; but they say that the bite of the scorpion and tarantula, though painful, is not dangerous to life. The nigua, (sometimes called chigua, and by the English corrupted into jigger,) is troublesome. With these exceptions, the claim to freedom from wild or venomous animals may be admitted. Their snakes are harmless, and the mosquitoes no worse than those of New England.

As to the climate, I have no doubt that in the interior, especially on the red earth, it is healthy and delightful, in summer as well as in winter; but on the river borders, in the low lands of black earth, and on the savannas, intermittent fever and fever-and-ague prevail. The cities have the scourge of yellow fever and, of late years, also the cholera. In the cities, I suppose, the year may be divided, as to sickness, into three equal portions: four months of winter, when they are safe; four of summer, when they are unsafe; and four of spring and autumn, when they are passing from one state to the other. There are, indeed, a few cases of vómito in the course of the winter, but they are little regarded, and must be the result of extreme imprudence. It is estimated that twenty-five per cent of the soldiers die of yellow fever the first years of their acclimation; and during the year of the cholera, sixty per cent of the newly-arrived soldiers died. The mean temperature in winter is 70 degrees, and in summer 83 degrees, Fahrenheit. The island has suffered severely from hurricanes, although they are not so frequent as in others of the West India islands. They have violent thunderstorms in summer, and have suffered from droughts in winter, though usually the heavy dews keep vegetation green through the dry season.

That which has been to me, personally, most unexpected, is the industry of the island. It seems to me that, allowing for the heat of noon and the debilitating effect of the climate, the industry in agriculture and trade is rather striking. The sugar crop is enormous. The annual exportation is about 400,000 tons, or about 2,000,000 boxes, and the amount consumed on the island is very great, not only in coffee and in daily cooking, but in the making of preserves and sweetmeats, which are a considerable part of the food of the people. There is also about half a million hogsheads of molasses exported annually. Add to this the coffee, tobacco and copper, and a general notion may be got of the industry and productions of the island. Its weak point is the want of variety. There are no manufactures of any consequence; the mineral exports are not great; and, in fact, sugar is the one staple. All Cuba has but one neck—the worst wish of the tyrant.

As to education, I have no doubt that a good education in medicine, and a respectable course of instruction in the Roman and Spanish law, and in the natural sciences, can be obtained at the University of Havana; and that a fair collegiate education, after the manner of the Latin races, can be obtained at the Jesuit College, the Seminario, and other institutions at Havana, and in the other large cities; and the Sisters of the Sacred Heart have a flourishing school for girls at Havana. But the general elementary education of the people is in a very low state. The scattered life of planters is unfavorable to public day-schools, nay, almost inconsistent with their existence. The richer inhabitants send their children abroad, or to Havana; but the middle and lower classes of whites cannot do this. The tables show that, of the free white children, not more than one in sixty-three attend any school, while in the British West India islands, the proportion is from one in ten to one in twenty. As to the state of education, culture and literary habits among the upper classes, my limited experience gives me no opportunity to judge. The concurrent testimony of tourists and other writers on Cuba is that the habits of the Cuban women of the upper and middle classes are unintellectual.

Education is substantially in the hands of the government. As an instance of their strictness, no man can take a degree at the University unless he makes oath that he does not belong to, has never belonged to, and will not belong to, any society not known to and permitted by the government.

REFLECTIONS

To return to the political state and prospects of Cuba. As for those persons whose political opinions and plans are not regulated by moral principle, it may be safely said that, whatever their plans, their object will not be the good of Cuba, but their own advantage. Of those who are governed by principle, each man's expectation or plan will depend upon the general opinion he entertains respecting the nature of men and of society. This is going back a good way for a test; but I am convinced it is only going to the source of opinion and action. If a man believes that human nature in an unrestrained course, is good, and self-governing, and that when it is not so, there is a temporary and local cause to be assigned for the deviation; if he believes that men, at least in civilized society, are independent beings, by right entitled to, and by nature capable of, the exercise of popular self-government, and that if they have not this power in exercise, it is because they have been deprived of it by somebody's fraud or violence, which ought to be detected and remedied, as we abate a public nuisance in the highway; if a man thinks that overturning a throne and erecting a constitution will answer the purpose;— if these are his opinions as to men and society, his plan for Cuba, and for every other part of the world, may be simple. No wonder such a one is impatient of the inactivity of the governed masses, and is in a constant state of surprise that the fraud and violence of a few should always prevail over the rights and merits of the many—when they themselves might end their thraldom by a blow, and put their oppressors to rest—by a bare bodkin!

But if the history of the world and the observation of his own times have led a man to the opinion that, of divine right and human necessity, government of some sort there must be, in which power must be vested somewhere, and exercised somehow; that popular self-government is rather of the nature of a faculty than of a right; that human nature is so constituted that the actual condition of civil society in any place and nation is, on the whole, the fair result of conflicting forces of good and evil—the power being in proportion to the need of power, and the franchises to the capacity for using franchises; that autocrats and oligarchs are the growth of the soil; and that every people has, in the main, and in the long run, a government as good as it deserves; if such is the substance of the belief to which he has been led or forced, he will look gravely upon the future of such people as the Cubans, and hesitate as to the invention and application of remedies. If he reflects that of all the nations of the southern races in North and South America, from Texas to Cape Horn, the Brazilians alone, who have a constitutional monarchy, are in a state of order and progress; and if he further reflects that Cuba, as a royal province, with all its evils, is in a better condition than nearly all the Spanish republican states, he may well be slow to believe that, with their complication of difficulties, and causes of disorder and weakness—with their half million or more of slaves and quarter million or less of free blacks, with their coolies, and their divided and hostile races of whites—their Spanish blood, and their utter want of experience in the discharge of any public duties, the Cubans will work out successfully the problem of self-government. You cannot reason from Massachusetts to Cuba. When Massachusetts entered into the Revolution, she had had one hundred and fifty years of experience in popular self-government under a system in which the exercise of this power was more generally diffused among the people, and extended over a larger class of subjects, and more decentralized, than had ever been known before in any part of the world, or at any period of the world's story. She had been, all along, for most purposes, an independent republic, with an obligation to the British Empire undefined and seldom attempted to be enforced. The thirteen colonies were ships fully armed and equipped, officered and manned, with long sea experience, sailing as a wing of a great fleet, under the Admiral's fleet signals. They had only to pass secret signals, fall out of line, haul their wind, and sail off as a squadron by themselves; and if the Admiral with the rest of the fleet made chase and gave battle, it was sailor to sailor and ship to ship. But Cuba has neither officers trained to the quarter-deck, nor sailors trained to the helm, the yard, or the gun. Nay, the ship is not built, nor the keel laid, nor is the timber grown, from which the keel is to be cut.

The natural process for Cuba is an amelioration of her institutions under Spanish auspices. If this is not to be had, or if the connection with Spain is dissolved in any way, she will probably be substantially under the protection of some other power, or a part of another empire. Whatever nation may enter upon such an undertaking as this, should take a bond of fate. Beside her internal danger and difficulties, Cuba is implicated externally with every cause of jealousy and conflict. She has been called the key to the Gulf of Mexico. But the Gulf of Mexico cannot be locked. Whoever takes her is more likely to find in her a key to Pandora's box. Close upon her is the great island of Jamaica, where the experiment of free Negro labor, in the same products, is on trial. Near to her is Haiti where the experiment of Negro self-government is on trial. And further off, separated, it is true, by the great Gulf Stream, and with the neighborhood of the almost uninhabited and uninhabitable sea coast of southern Florida, yet near enough to furnish some cause for uneasiness, are the slave-states of the Great Republic. She is an island, too; and as an island, whatever power holds or protects her, must maintain on the spot a sufficient army and navy, as it would not do to rely upon being able to throw in troops and munitions of war, after notice of need.

As to the wishes of the Cubans themselves, the degree of reliance they place, or are entitled to place, on each other, and their opportunities and capacity for organized action of any kind, I have already set down all I can be truly said to know; and there is no end to assertion and conjecture, or to the conflicting character of what is called information, whether received through men or books.

XXII

LEAVE-TAKING

All day there have been earnest looks to the northwest, for the smoke of the "Cahawba." We are willing and desirous to depart. Our sights are seen, our business done, and our trunks packed. While we are sitting round our table after dinner, George, Mr. Miller's servant, comes in, with a bright countenance, and says "There is a steamer off." We go to the roof, and there, far in the N. W., is a small but unmistakable cloud of steamer's smoke, just in the course the "Cahawba" would take. "Let us walk down to the Punta, and see her come in." It is between four and five o'clock, and a pleasant afternoon, and we saunter along, keeping in the shade, and sit down on the boards at the wharf, in front of the Presidio, near to where politicians are garroted, and watch the progress of the steamer, amusing ourselves at the same time with seeing the Negroes swimming and washing horses in the shallow water off the bank. A Yankee flag flies from the signalpost of the Morro, but the Punta keeps the steamer from our sight. It draws towards six o'clock, and no vessel can enter after dark. We begin to fear she will not reach the point in season. Her cloud of smoke rises over the Punta, the city clocks strike six, the Morro strikes six, the trumpets bray out, the sun is down, the signals on the Morro are lowering—"She'll miss it!"—"No—there she is!"—and, round the Punta comes her sharp black head, and then her full body, her toiling engine and smoking chimney and peopled decks, and flying stars and stripes—Good luck to her! and, though the signal is down, she pushes on and passes the forts without objection, and is lost among the shipping.

My companions are so enthusiastic that they go on board; but I return to my hotel and take a volante, and make my last calls, and take my last looks, and am ready to leave in the morning.

In half an hour, the arrival of the "Cahawba" is known over all Havana, and the news of the loss of her consort, the "Black Warrior," in a fog off New York—passengers and crew and specie safe. My companions come back. They met Capt. Bullock on the pier, and took tea with him in La Dominica. He sails at two o'clock to-morrow.

I shall not see them again, but there they will be, day after day, day after day—how long?—aye, how long?—the squalid, degraded chain-gang! The horrible prison!—profaning one of the grandest of sites, where city, sea and shore unite as almost nowhere else on earth! These were my thoughts as, in the pink and gray dawn, I walked down the Paseo, to enjoy my last refreshing in the rock-hewn sea-baths.

This leave-taking is a strange process, and has strange effects. How suddenly a little of unnoticed good in what you leave behind comes out, and touches you, in a moment of tenderness! And how much of the evil and disagreeable seems to have disappeared! Le Grand, after all, is no more inattentive and intractable than many others would become in his place; and he does keep a good table, and those breakfasts are very pretty. Antonio is no hydropathist, to be sure, and his ear distinguishes the voices that pay best; yet one pities him in his routine, and in the fear he is under, being a native of Old Spain, that his name will turn up in the conscription, when he will have to shoulder his musket for five years in the Cabaña and Punta. Nor can he get off the island, for the permit will be refused him, poor fellow!

One or two of our friends are to remain here for they have pulmonary difficulties, and prefer to avoid the North in March. They look a little sad at being left alone, and talk of going into the country to escape the increasing heat. A New York gentleman has taken a great fancy to the volantes, and thinks that a costly one, with two horses, and silvered postilion in boots and spurs and bright jacket would eclipse any equipage in Fifth Avenue.

When you come to leave, you find that the strange and picturesque character of the city has interested you more than you think; and you stare out of your carriage to read the familiar signs, the names of streets, the Obra Pia, Lamparilla, Mercaderes, San Ignacio, Obispo, O'Reilly, and Oficios, and the pretty and fantastic names of the shops. You think even the narrow streets have their advantages, as they are better shaded, and the awnings can stretch across them, though, to be sure, they keep out the air. No city has finer avenues than the Isabel and the Tacón; and the palm trees, at least, we shall not see at the North. Here is La Dominica. It is a pleasant place, in the evening, after the Retreta, to take your tea or coffee under the trees by the fountain in the court-yard, and meet the Americans and English—the only public place, except the theater, where ladies are to be seen out of their volantes. Still, we are quite ready to go; for we have seen all we have been told to see in Havana, and it is excessively hot, and growing hotter.

But no one can leave Cuba without a permit. When you arrive, the visé of your passport is not enough, but you must pay a fee for a permit to land and remain in the island; and when you wish to return, you must pay four dollars to get back your passport, with a permit to leave. The custom-house officials were not troublesome in respect to our luggage, hardly examining it at all, and, I must admit, showed no signs of expecting private fees. Along the range of piers, where the bows of the vessels run in, and on which the labor of this great commerce is performed, there runs a high, wide roof, covering all from the intense rays of the sun. Before this was put up, they say that workmen used to fall dead with sunstrokes, on the wharves.

On board the "Cahawba," I find my barrel of oranges from Iglesia, and box of sweet-meats from La Dominica, and boxes of cigars from Cabaña's, punctually delivered. There, once more, is Bullock, cheerful, and efficient; Rodgers, full of kindness and good-humor; and sturdy, trustworthy Miller, and Porter, the kindly and spirited; and the pleased face of Henry, the captain's steward; and the familiar faces of the other stewards; and my friend's son, who is well and very glad to see me, and full of New Orleans, and of last night, which he spent on shore in Havana. All are in good spirits, for a short sea voyage with old friends is before us; and then—home!

The decks are loaded and piled up with oranges: oranges in barrels and oranges in crates, filling all the wings and gangways, the barrels cut to let in air, and the crates with bars just close enough to keep in the oranges. The delays from want of lighters, and the great amount of freight, keep us through the day; and it is nearly sundown before we get under way. All day the fruit boats are along-side, and passengers and crew lay in stocks of oranges and bananas and sapotes, and little boxes of sweetmeats. At length, the last barrel is on board, the permits and passenger-lists are examined, the revenue officers leave us, and we begin to heave up our anchor.

The harbor is very full of vessels, and the room for swinging is small. A British mail-steamer, and a Spanish man-of-war, and several merchantmen, are close upon us. Captain Bullock takes his second mate aft and they have a conference, as quietly as if they were arranging a funeral. He is explaining to him his plan for running the warps and swinging the ship, and telling him beforehand what he is to do in this case, and what in that, and how to understand his signs, so that no orders, or as few as possible, need be given at the time of action. The engine moves, the warp is hauled upon, the anchor tripped, and dropped again, and tripped again, the ship takes the right sheer, clear of everything, and goes handsomely out of the harbor, the stars and stripes at her peak, with a waving of hats from friends on the Punta wharf. The western sky is gorgeous with the setting sun, and the evening drums and trumpets sound from the encircling fortifications, as we pass the Casa Blanca, the Cabaña, the Punta, and the Morro. The sky fades, the ship rises and falls in the heave of the sea, the lantern of the Morro gleams over the water, and the dim shores of Cuba are hidden from our sight.

Milton Keynes UK
Ingram Content Group UK Ltd.
UKHW011144220424
441551UK00007B/809